Why a Daughter Needs a Good Dad

The Lifelong Impact of a Father's Love and Guidance

Elizabeth Parke

© Copyright 2024 - All rights reserved.

The content contained within this book may not be reproduced, duplicated or transmitted without direct written permission from the author or the publisher.

Under no circumstances will any blame or legal responsibility be held against the publisher, or author, for any damages, reparation, or monetary loss due to the information contained within this book, either directly or indirectly.

Legal Notice:

This book is copyright protected. It is only for personal use. You cannot amend, distribute, sell, use, quote or paraphrase any part, or the content within this book, without the consent of the author or publisher.

Disclaimer Notice:

Please note the information contained within this document is for educational and entertainment purposes only. All effort has been executed to present accurate, up to date, reliable, complete information. No warranties of any kind are declared or implied. Readers acknowledge that the author is not engaged in the rendering of legal, financial, medical or professional advice. The content within this book has been derived from various sources. Please consult a licensed professional before attempting any techniques outlined in this book.

By reading this document, the reader agrees that under no circumstances is the author responsible for any losses, direct or indirect, that are incurred as a result of the use of the information contained within this document, including, but not limited to, errors, omissions, or inaccuracies.

Table of Contents

INTRODUCTION 1

CHAPTER 1: THE FOUNDATION OF A STRONG RELATIONSHIP 3

   THE ROLE OF A FATHER IN A DAUGHTER'S EARLY YEARS 4
      The Importance of Connection 4
      Creating Lifelong Bonds 5
      Trust as a Security Base 5
   ESTABLISHING TRUST AND EMOTIONAL SECURITY 7
      The Role of Active Listening 7
      Navigating Conflict With Trust 8
   PRACTICAL TIPS FOR BUILDING A STRONG BOND 9
      Creating Memories and Exploring Mutual Interests 9
      Setting the Tone for Conversation 10

CHAPTER 2: THE POWER OF A FATHER'S LOVE 13

   HOW A FATHER'S (OR STEPFATHER'S) LOVE SHAPES A DAUGHTER'S SELF-WORTH 13
      Building Self-Esteem 14
      Encouragement Through Challenges 14
      Promoting Future Success 16
      Recognizing Different Emotions 16
      Modeling Emotional Regulation 17
   ACTIONABLE ADVICE FOR FATHERS TO EXPRESS LOVE EFFECTIVELY 18
      Understanding Love Languages 18
      Verbal Affirmations 20
      Seeking Feedback and Creating Traditions 21

CHAPTER 3: THE CONSEQUENCES OF ABSENCE OR NEGLECT 23

   HOW AN ABSENT FATHER AFFECTS A DAUGHTER: A FIRSTHAND LOOK 23
   THE PSYCHOLOGICAL IMPACT OF FATHERLY NEGLECT 26
      Attachment Theory and Father-Daughter Relationships 26
      How a Father Shapes His Daughter's Self-Worth 27
      Recommendations for Healing and Rebuilding Relationships 28
   LONG-TERM EFFECTS OF AN ABSENT FATHER ON MENTAL HEALTH AND
   RELATIONSHIP CHOICES 29
      Adverse Father-Daughter Interactions and Mental Health 29
      Relationship Choices and Unhealthy Patterns 30

CHAPTER 4: THE ROLE OF A FATHER IN BUILDING CONFIDENCE 33

Encouraging Independence and Resilience 33
How Fathers Can Foster Independence 34
Fathers' Role in Building Resilience... 35
The Importance of Supporting a Daughter's Ambitions 36
How Fathers Can Validate Their Daughters' Ambitions................ 37
The Long-Term Impact of Fatherly Support................................. 38
Snapshots of Success 39

CHAPTER 5: HOW GOOD DADS SHAPE HEALTHY RELATIONSHIPS 43

A Father's Influence on His Daughter's Partner.................................... 44
Father-Daughter Interactions, Emotional Foundations, and Relationship Expectations.. 44
Fathers and the Standard They Set.. 45
Fatherly Examples and Preventing Abusive Relationships 47
What Dads Teach Their Daughters About Boundaries and Respect............ 48
Recognizing Red Flags and the Need to Maintain Independence................ 49
Real-Life Relationships: Showcasing a Father's Gift 50

CHAPTER 6: RAISING INDEPENDENT DAUGHTERS 53

The Importance of Financial Independence.. 53
Imparting Basic Financial Literacy... 54
Education as a Means to Independence 57
Teaching Daughters to Value Themselves 59
A Father's Role in Helping His Daughter Appreciate Her Strengths............ 59
Helping Daughters Prepare for Life Transitions............................ 60

CHAPTER 7: THE QUIET STRENGTH OF CONSISTENCY 63

A Consistent Presence Builds Lasting Security.................................... 63
Measurable Outcomes Due to Consistency................................. 64
The Role of Routine in Stable Relationships....................................... 65
Creating a Consistent, Predictable Routine 66
The Father-Daughter Relationship and Work-Life Balance 70

CHAPTER 8: GROWING TOGETHER—THE EVOLUTION OF THE FATHER-DAUGHTER RELATIONSHIP.. 73

Adapting to Different Stages of Life 74
Early Childhood... 74
Adolescence 75
Young Adulthood 76
How Father-Daughter Bonds Change as Daughters Grow Older 76
Maintaining a Strong Relationship Into Adulthood............................. 79

CHAPTER 9: THE LEGACY OF A GOOD DAD 83
THE LONG-TERM IMPACT OF A FATHER'S LOVE 83
A Father's Influence on Generational Cycles *84*
GOOD DADS INFLUENCE THEIR DAUGHTERS' PARENTING 86
THE LASTING IMPRINT OF A FATHER'S GUIDANCE 88

CHAPTER 10: LESSONS FOR FATHERS—HOW TO BE THE BEST DAD YOU CAN BE 91
ADVICE FOR CURRENT AND FUTURE FATHERS 91
SETTING FAIR, RESPECTFUL BOUNDARIES 95
CONTINUAL IMPROVEMENT AS A FATHER 97
Further Resources *98*

CONCLUSION 101

REFERENCES 105

Introduction

No one in this world can love a girl more than her father.
–Michael Ratnadeepak

When I was a nurse working in mental health, I met a young woman named Emma. She was in her late twenties, with tired eyes and a hesitant smile that hinted at the weight she carried. Emma was intelligent, articulate, and deeply compassionate. But underneath her calm exterior was a storm of self-doubt, anxiety, and a longing she couldn't quite put into words.

Over several conversations, Emma opened up about her childhood. Her father had been physically present but emotionally absent. He worked long hours, often came home exhausted, and rarely engaged with her. When he did, it was usually to criticize her for something she'd done wrong—a poor grade, a messy room, or an attitude he didn't approve of. Emma learned early on that seeking his approval was like chasing a mirage.

As she grew older, Emma carried this invisible wound into her relationships. She dated men who mirrored her father—distant, dismissive, and emotionally unavailable. Each breakup felt like confirmation of what she feared most: she wasn't good enough to be loved.

But then there was Sarah, another young woman I had the chance to meet around the same time. Sarah's father wasn't perfect—no father is—but he showed up for her in all the ways that mattered. He asked about her day, listened when she spoke, and made her feel like her voice mattered. He attended her school plays, cheered her on at soccer games, and was a steady presence in her life.

The difference in these two women's stories was stark. Sarah carried herself with a quiet confidence. She believed in her worth and wasn't afraid to set boundaries in her relationships. She faced challenges with resilience because, deep down, she knew she was loved and valued.

These stories aren't unique. In my years working in medicine, I've seen countless versions of Emma and Sarah. The father-daughter relationship is one of the most powerful and underestimated bonds in a girl's life. It shapes how she sees herself, how she interacts with the world, and how she loves and allows herself to be loved.

This book isn't about placing blame or pointing fingers. It's about awareness, healing, and growth. Whether you're a father hoping to build or rebuild a relationship with your daughter, a mother supporting that bond, or an adult woman reflecting on your own father-daughter story, this book is for you.

In the chapters ahead, you'll find real stories, practical advice, and insights into the emotional and psychological impact of a father's presence—or absence—in his daughter's life.

Let's begin this journey together. Because every daughter deserves a father who shows up, stays present, and loves her in a way that shapes her life for the better.

Chapter 1:

The Foundation of a Strong Relationship

A good father will leave his imprint on his daughter for the rest of her life.
–Dr. James Dobson

Creating trust within the father-daughter relationship starts from day one. Fathers may not realize it, but they're laying the foundation for their bond with their daughter from the very first time they pick her up. Establishing trust and a secure attachment from the start is one of the greatest gifts that a father can give their young daughter.

In this chapter, we'll explore the role that a father plays in his daughter's early years and why this initial establishment of trust is so crucial for a healthy father-daughter relationship to form. I'll illustrate how strong emotional bonds between fathers and daughters can serve as the cornerstone for the daughter's overall development and well-being.

But this chapter isn't just packed full of theory. We'll also look at practical tips for fathers who want to build a strong bond with their daughter and what fathers can do to solidify their relationship with their daughter starting from an early age. Even fathers who, for one reason or another, were unable to form a strong connection with their daughter during her early life can still start to implement some of these ideas to bridge the gap and start to rebuild the relationship.

The Role of a Father in a Daughter's Early Years

The bond between a father and daughter starts right away, and the first decade of the daughter's life is a crucial time for building their relationship. These are the years when connection and bonding establish a strong foundation of trust. As one pair of researchers found, a parent's love, support, and time are the most valuable gifts that they can give to a child (Winston & Chicot, 2016). Providing this love and support, as well as prioritizing time with the daughter, will lay the groundwork for a healthy father-daughter relationship in the years to come.

The Importance of Connection

When a father creates a secure attachment with his daughter, they form an emotional bond. This bond, in turn, helps foster trust and stability. When the daughter is securely attached to her father, she feels valued and understood. She trusts in her father's presence, and she has a secure foundation from which to launch future relationships.

This emotional connection also influences a daughter's ability to manage stress and face challenges effectively. Science has shown us that we actually learn how to deal with stress very early in life, before we even turn four. In these formative years, cortisol levels are quite high as we learn to control our mood, face down our fears, and figure out what motivates us (Roberts, 2020). The rough-and-tumble type of play that dads often encourage helps teach their daughters how to approach a challenge in a way that stays within safe boundaries, and this also means they learn how to regulate their reactions and handle the stress that comes along with taking a risk.

A lack of emotional bonding can lead to feelings of inadequacy and even affect the daughter's interpersonal skills. She doubts her self-worth, because she wonders if there is something "wrong" with her that has prevented her father from forming a relationship with her. In contrast, a strong father-daughter relationship promotes feelings of self-worth in the daughter. She's able to explore her identity without fear of being judged, and she's confident that others will love her just the way she is thanks to the trust she has in her father's unconditional love.

Creating Lifelong Bonds

Strong emotional connections create a lasting relationship that evolves over time. The father and daughter share a foundation of mutual respect and understanding, and they navigate life together as a team rather than seeing each other as adversaries. The early years are crucial, but remember that the goal isn't just to bond for the daughter's first decade; it's to create a bond that is built for a lifetime.

Daughters are more likely to seek advice and guidance from their father if they have formed a strong bond. At first, as the bond is forming and the daughter is young, they might need their father to guide them in how to tie their shoes, ride a bike, or tackle their math homework. These small, low-stakes scenarios pave the way for the daughter to naturally seek out her father's advice later in life when they're facing situations with higher stakes, such as financial and professional decisions.

Trust as a Security Base

When daughters feel that they're in a trusting environment, they're able to explore their world without fear of judgement. To help create this type of environment, fathers can work to practice authoritative parenting.

In brief, researchers have classified parenting into four distinct styles: authoritarian, permissive, neglectful, and authoritative. Authoritarian parenting is best summed up as the "drill sergeant dad," who has strict rules and expects to be obeyed at all costs (and doles out regular punishments for any infraction). Permissive parents function more as their child's friend than as their parent. The child has a lot of freedom and is encouraged to do what they like, and boundaries are rarely enforced. The neglectful parent meets their child's basic needs for food, shelter, and clothing, but has little emotional involvement in their life. This is the stereotypical "absent dad" who's constantly working or traveling for work and spends very little time with their child. Finally, authoritative parenting is typically considered the most desirable parenting model because authoritative parents set clear boundaries while also providing their children with love, respect, and trust. The authoritative parent is involved in their child's life and has rules in place that promote the child's well-being and development, but they're also willing to be flexible and show understanding when circumstances dictate.

There are a multitude of resources about these four parenting styles available, and learning more about what it means to be an authoritative parent is worth every father's time. Intentionally thinking about words and actions to work toward authoritative parenting helps fathers to develop caring relationships with their daughters. The daughter can trust that her father wants to be a part of her life, cares about her physical and emotional well-being, and is available to listen to her needs.

Taking the time to practice authoritative parenting helps to build trust and facilitates open communication. This makes it easier for daughters to share their successes and concerns with their father. They know that being with their dad is a safe space, and they'll be loved and cherished no matter what they reveal.

In contrast, a loss of trust can lead to long-term relational issues. This is something we'll explore much more deeply in Chapter 5, but the research has shown that girls who don't have a healthy relationship with their father are much more likely to experience negative relationships with others later in life (*The Importance of Father Daughter Relationships*, 2019). Thus, establishing trust early—and putting in the effort to maintain it—is crucial.

Establishing Trust and Emotional Security

When fathers are emotionally available, it teaches their daughters that their emotions are valuable, valid, and worth communicating to others. This, in turn, builds security and trust. Being emotionally available, though, is something that doesn't always come naturally to fathers. A little knowledge about active listening and navigating conflict without fracturing relationships can be invaluable when it comes to helping fathers establish trust with their daughters.

The Role of Active Listening

Active listening is one of the best ways for a father to show his daughter that he's emotionally available and invested in what she has to say. Active listening means being an intentional part of a conversation, rather than simply and passively allowing the other person's words to wash over you. Active listeners are attentive and make it their goal to understand what the other person truly means and where they're coming from. They also take the time to reflect on what's been said before responding, and they remember what was said even after the conversation is over.

When a father practices active listening, it helps his daughter feel respected and valued. She's more likely to share openly when she knows her father is paying attention to her words instead of just nodding his head while he focuses on something else. That also means she's more likely to talk with him about touchy subjects. She'll feel safe enough to bring up uncomfortable or challenging topics because she trusts that her dad is truly hearing what she has to say and will reflect on her words before responding.

Dads who listen actively can converse with their daughters on a deeper level. Their interactions aren't limited to conversations like "How was your day?" "Oh, okay. How about yours?" "It was fine." Instead, a father who actively listens will pick up on the nuance of "Oh, okay" to hear the lack of enthusiasm in his daughter's voice and realize that she's not her usual bubbly self. He'll realize he needs to probe a bit deeper to find out what happened in her day and ask if she needs any support or guidance. This also gives fathers the chance to model problem-solving skills by talking through challenges with their daughters and helping them figure out a solution, rather than just telling their daughter what to do and solving the problem for her.

In turn, a daughter whose dad picks up on her subtle cues and listens for the real meaning of her words feels emotionally secure. She's willing to open up because she knows her father truly cares, and she doesn't have to hide behind a brave face and pretend like everything's fine, whether it is or not. Her father may not be perfect, but he tries his best to understand her—and that's what really counts.

Navigating Conflict With Trust

Even the best relationships sometimes encounter conflict, so being prepared for the inevitable rocky patches that will arise helps ensure that fathers and daughters can keep their bond intact even when there's a disagreement. Remember that with any conflict, the goal isn't to convince one person to come around to the other's way of thinking. It's to collaborate jointly to find a resolution, and to respect both people's viewpoints, ideas, and opinions along the way.

When fathers and daughters experience conflict, it can actually lead to a relationship that is ultimately stronger and more trusting. Conflict challenges a relationship and forces both people to look more closely at their thoughts and how they're communicating with the other person. Often, that can be uncomfortable for one or both people. Sadly, sometimes this results in one person shutting down or closing themself off and refusing to consider any kind of change. As a result, the relationship generally suffers.

But other times, both people are willing to look objectively at the situation and work through the conflict together. This creates emotional security, because the father and daughter both see that the other person isn't backing away even though things might be tough. It also creates a deeper bond because they are collaborating to resolve the situation and are willing to respectfully consider the other person's viewpoint.

This is particularly important for daughters. It can be easy for a father to "bulldoze" his daughter and assert his will, as her parent, regardless of her feelings. By taking the time to talk and truly listen, the father can understand where his daughter is coming from and consider any compromises that may be made. He may need to make decisions to protect her health and safety that she doesn't like, such as instituting a particular curfew or establishing certain rules around driving privileges. But because he's shown that he cares about her viewpoint and her feelings, she can feel confident that he has her best interests at heart and has genuinely considered her before making the decision.

Practical Tips for Building a Strong Bond

Building a lifelong bond through active listening may sound well and good, but many fathers find it hard to know how to get started. They may strongly desire to connect with their daughters, if they only knew what to do or say. The good news is that building a strong bond isn't as challenging as many fathers think. To close out the chapter, I'll share a few practical, tried-and-true tips that any father can put into practice to strengthen their relationship with their daughter.

Creating Memories and Exploring Mutual Interests

One of the best ways to strengthen any relationship is to share an experience, and this is true for the father-daughter bond, too. Engaging in activities together results in a shared experience that will solidify the relationship, no matter what the activity might be. Many daughters, once they're adults, cite these shared activities as some of the best memories of their childhood. I know one woman who has extremely vivid and fond memories of her dad taking her for rides around the yard in their wheelbarrow when she was a young child, and another woman who affectionately remembers riding along in her dad's truck and playing the alphabet game with road signs when he went on work-related errands. An experience doesn't have to be particularly exciting or dramatic to make a major impact.

Doing school drop-off or pick-up as often as the dad's schedule allows is a great way to spend time together, and adding a fun element like turning the music up to sing along or stopping on the way for a hot chocolate can solidify the memory. Going out for ice cream, taking a bike ride, learning a new dance move from a YouTube how-to video, or picking out wacky outfits for each other from the thrift store and then wearing them to dinner are just a small sampling of ways to share an experience and strengthen a relationship. For many dads, doing something active with their daughters feels like the easiest way to get started. Taking a walk, going on a bike ride, and raking the leaves together all count as quality father-daughter time—especially if they're accompanied with conversation.

When dads take the time to find out what their daughter is interested in and then learn about that thing, it shows their daughter they're loved and cared for in a very powerful way. If the daughter has a favorite singer or band, her father could learn their music so they can belt it out at the top of their lungs together. Maybe she's passionate about a particular sport; he can learn the rules, if he doesn't already know them, and offer to help her practice. Perhaps art is her thing, and they could take a painting class together or visit a local art show to see different artists' work.

The options are endless, and the ideas shared here provide ideas to start with but are by no means comprehensive. Father-daughter activities can be fun outings that are planned in advance, spur-of-the-moment jaunts, or routine tasks that are livened up by being shared. The goal is to have periodic times where a father intentionally carves out time to spend with his daughter and conveys, through the gift of his time and attention, how much he loves and supports her.

Setting the Tone for Conversation

While conversation often comes more easily to girls than to their fathers, it shouldn't be the daughter's job to constantly initiate communication. Fathers have a responsibility to engage with their daughters regularly, and the tone and frequency of their conversation often depends on how the father approaches the interaction.

When a father keeps his attitude open and non-judgmental, it allows his daughter to express herself without fear. His communication style has a big impact on how her own interpersonal skills will develop, so it's important to model healthy communication. That means conversing with the daughter on a regular basis and in a variety of ways.

Some conversations can and should be lighthearted and playful. I have one friend who often played a game with her father called "Would You Rather," where they'd ask each other ridiculous questions like "Would you rather have very long arms that dragged on the ground when you walked or tiny short arms that barely reached the ground?" and then laugh as the other person tried to justify their answer.

Other conversations will need to be more serious or educational, like conversations about handling finances or the repercussions of behaving a certain way in a certain situation. Many conversations will fall somewhere in between: not exactly silly, but not exactly solemn, either—like a discussion of how well their favorite sports team is doing this year, or what they both thought of the movie they watched last week.

One of the best ways for fathers to make sure they're making enough time for conversation with their daughters is to make regular weekly check-ins a part of their routine. The ritual could feel very elaborate, like going to the local coffee shop every Monday afternoon and sitting down together, or fairly informal, like walking the dog together right before bed. The important thing is that the conversation is occurring on a regular basis and is a priority in the father's life. This also helps keep the lines of communication open even as daughters grow into difficult times of their life where talking with their dad could feel awkward or cringe-inducing if it's not already part of their regular routine.

When fathers spend time with their daughters and make regular conversation a priority, it goes a long way toward fostering their daughter's healthy sense of self-worth, creating resilience, and building an affectionate relationship. In our next chapter, we'll look at the powerful impact of a father's love in greater detail.

Chapter 2:

The Power of a Father's Love

When my father didn't have my hand, he had my back.
—Linda Poindexter

Experiencing a father's love has massive impacts on a daughter's life. It fosters healthy self-worth and resilience as well as setting her up for success later in life by equipping her to tackle challenges confidently. Many dads who love their daughters deeply often struggle to outwardly indicate the depth of their love. As a result, their daughters may be slow to realize how much they're loved. As we talk about the power of a father's love, I'll share anecdotes to illustrate just how important it is for daughters to understand and experience their father's love for them. I'll also provide some simple, straightforward ideas to help fathers better verbalize and demonstrate the way they feel about their daughter.

How a Father's (Or Stepfather's) Love Shapes a Daughter's Self-Worth

Positive reinforcement from a father or stepfather has a big impact on their daughter's emotional and psychological well-being. While dads may not think their words and actions matter much, over time, each interaction adds up to either contribute to or eat away at their daughter's self-esteem. A father's love also helps his daughter to learn effective emotional regulation and how to recognize different feelings.

Building Self-Esteem

A father or stepfather's regular praise and verbal affirmation can significantly enhance his daughter's self-esteem. When he acknowledges her strengths and achievements, it affirms her sense of self-worth. Consistent positive reinforcement creates an upward feedback loop, where the daughter believes in her own abilities and is more likely to succeed in her future attempts as a result. A solid self-esteem also lays the groundwork for healthy relationships and decision-making later in life.

Fathers don't have to wait until their daughters are in elementary school and beyond before starting to build up their self-esteem, either. Research has shown that starting around two years of age, fathers have a powerful impact on the development of self-doubt in their daughters. Remarkably, ages two through four are some of the most important years for fathers to encourage their daughters in trying new things and learning new skills (Langlois, 2014). This has a massive impact on self-esteem because girls who are encouraged to explore their world and whose newly learned skills are celebrated develop greater autonomy, which translates into higher self-esteem and less self-doubt.

In contrast, fathers who ignore or restrict their daughters' exploration and skill-building during these formative years can create self-doubt because the daughter starts to question her ability to learn things and master new skill sets. Their daughters feel unimportant, and so they don't view their interests and abilities as important, either. They constantly feel the need to seek reassurance from others because they don't feel confident in their skills.

Encouragement Through Challenges

Just as a father has a huge impact on their daughter's self-esteem—or lack thereof—he also has an outsized role when it comes to building her confidence to successfully navigate challenges. Positive reinforcement from the father gives the daughter courage and hope, while a lack of support leaves daughters feeling isolated and ill-equipped to tackle any hardships they may face.

I'd like to note that encouraging someone to navigate a challenge doesn't equate to solving the problem for them. While many dads are wired to solve problems for the people they love, that can actually hold their daughter back in the long run because she'll end up feeling helpless and like she needs someone who can take care of her. Instead, a father should provide reassurance that the daughter is capable of facing down difficulties and will be able to overcome hardships with persistence and creativity. Dads can also share techniques or tools and have brainstorming sessions with their daughter to jump-start ideas for problem-solving. There are many ways fathers can offer support without taking over and solving the problem for their daughter.

For instance, let me share a story about my college roommate, who I'll call "Jane." A few weeks into our freshman year, we tried to hop in the car to get some ice cream. The only problem? Her old Toyota Camry wouldn't start. Jane immediately called her dad to find out what she should do. I listened as her dad, who I'll call "Steve," started to help Jane problem-solve. The first thing he did was say, "Well, what do you think you should do, honey?" Jane thought for a moment and then slowly stated, "I'm on your Triple-A membership, right? Can I call Triple-A?" Steve affirmed this idea, telling her that's exactly what he would have done. Next, Jane asked him what the Triple-A number was. Steve replied, "Is the Triple-A card that I gave you during move-in weekend in your wallet?" Jane indicated that it was. Steve next asked, "Have you taken a look at the card?" Jane pulled it out quickly and scanned both sides of the card. We could both see that the card had a phone number printed on it, along with her membership information. Jane asked a few follow-up questions about what to tell Triple-A and how long it would take them to arrive. Steve gave her a quick overview of what to expect and suggested that she should find out if there was a local Toyota dealership where she could have Triple-A tow her car, if they couldn't get it started. While I waited in the car for the tow truck to arrive, she ran back up to our room to do a quick online search for area dealerships (this was before smartphones were ubiquitous and you had to use a computer to search the internet!).

The Triple-A repairman was able to jumpstart her Camry that day, but it blew a tire a few months later. This time, though, Jane was ready to jump into action. She knew exactly what to do and didn't even bother to call Steve first. His encouragement in helping her figure out what to do for herself was highly effective, and she was confident in her ability to handle her car issues from then on.

Promoting Future Success

In addition to helping daughters learn to problem-solve, a father's positive reinforcement can actually cultivate a thirst for knowledge in their daughters. When the daughter is encouraged to try new things, she's more likely to take calculated risks so that she can fully explore her potential. This, in turn, fosters lifelong learning and the ability to adapt—two traits that are critical for success in modern society.

Daughters whose efforts are encouraged are also more likely to provide positive reinforcement to others.

Recognizing Different Emotions

When fathers encourage daughters to identify and articulate their feelings, it can help them understand emotional nuances. While mothers are typically thought of as being more emotionally attuned than fathers, several studies have found a link between fathers and emotional regulation in children, indicating that dads actually play a crucial role in teaching daughters that all emotions are valid and deserve acknowledgement (Islamiah et al., 2023).

When emotions are acknowledged, self-awareness increases, and girls are better able to manage their emotions effectively in various situations. This helps them to navigate challenges with clarity and composure.

One way that fathers can help their daughters learn to recognize and regulate emotions in the early years is actually through physical play. Research has shown that when dads roughhouse and play with their daughter, she becomes emotionally overstimulated (Islamiah et al., 2023). She can then practice regulating those emotions in a setting that's safe where her father is available to offer guidance. The father's support is key here, as children who roughhoused with their father but were not given any emotional direction actually failed to learn how to regulate emotional overstimulation.

Using positive parenting techniques is another way that fathers can help their daughters learn to regulate their emotions, as fathers who used harsh parenting practices or who were emotionally unavailable were shown to have children with lower ability to regulate their emotions (Islamiah et al., 2023). In short, dads should play with their daughters and help them practice naming, acknowledging, and managing their emotions as part of their play.

Modeling Emotional Regulation

As part of daughters' journeys toward learning emotional regulation, it's important for their fathers to model what that looks like. When a father can demonstrate a healthy emotional response, even in a challenging situation, their daughter is more likely to be able to do the same. This emotional modeling starts from the time that the daughter is very young. For instance, researchers have identified that when a dad is wrestling or engaging in rough-and-tumble play with his children and then finishes the play and calmly handles a household chore, it shows their children how to switch their emotional intensity based on the situation and what types of emotional responses are appropriate in different situations (Tift, 2019).

It can often be helpful for a father to verbalize their emotional response, especially when the daughter is young. While this might feel uncomfortable for many dads at first, it really helps their daughter see how they're choosing a healthy reaction even if it goes against their natural tendency. For instance, if the father is frustrated about a work-related email he has just received, he might say something like, "I'm really upset about this situation at work, but I know that getting angry at my co-worker won't help things. I'm going to go mow the yard and take some time to cool down before I answer him."

Daughters who see their fathers remain calm even when they experience ups and downs develop more resilience, because they understand that peaks and valleys are a part of life. They're able to develop similar coping mechanisms because they've seen their father model a healthy emotional response, and this is a trait that will serve them well later in life.

Actionable Advice for Fathers to Express Love Effectively

Since outward expressions of love don't always come naturally to fathers, I want to share some actionable steps that fathers can take to make sure their daughters know they're loved. Showing love to a daughter doesn't have to involve a grand, over-the-top gesture. Understanding what makes the daughter feel loved and appreciated, affirming her verbally, and taking time to create traditions with her are all important ways that fathers can demonstrate to their daughters just how precious they are.

Understanding Love Languages

Dr. Gary Chapman, a counselor and bestselling author, is perhaps best-known for his book *The 5 Love Languages*. In the book, Chapman outlines five different primary ways that people show and receive love. He calls each of these five ways a "love language" and theorizes that people feel most loved when they receive love in their primary language. While Chapman's book was originally written for couples in a romantic relationship, he's also authored a book on love languages for children, and his ideas have been expanded to include all types of close relationships, not just romantic ones.

Under Chapman's model, the five love languages include

- **acts of service**: doing things that serve the other person without being asked
- **physical touch**: loving, affectionate physical contact

- **quality time**: spending time together and giving the other person your undivided attention

- **receiving gifts**: giving the other person a gift or memento that lets them know you were thinking of them

- **words of affirmation**: speaking words that affirm and uplift the other person

When fathers take time to learn about the love languages and identify their daughter's primary love language, it will help them tailor their interactions accordingly. If a daughter values quality time, a father might make sure to set aside time when the two of them could run errands together or play a board game. If she loves receiving gifts, her dad could occasionally pick up a muffin from her favorite bakery on his way home from work. Small actions spoken in her love language really help to make a daughter feel incredibly loved and valued.

I know a dad who was able to radically transform his relationship with his eight-year-old daughter simply by starting to "speak her language." The dad, whom I'll call Mike, was introduced to the love languages and started thinking about how often his daughter, who I'll call Lila, begged to go with him on errands or help him complete household chores. He usually brushed her off, and then her whole demeanor would turn sour and stay that way. Thanks to his newfound knowledge about the love languages, Mike realized that his daughter felt loved when someone gave her the gift of quality time.

He started saying "yes" instead of "no" when she asked to ride along while he did errands or tag along when he was working around the house. Lila began going with him to buy dog food, take her older brothers to soccer practice, or pick up the pizza for their weekly family movie night. Mike also let Lila start helping him rake leaves, wash the dishes, sweep up the kitchen floor after dinner, and assist with other similar chores. At first, Lila seemed a little unsure and didn't know exactly what to make of the sudden change. But within a week or two, it was like a switch had flipped. Lila was constantly upbeat, with none of the pouting or grumbling that had previously characterized her conversations with Mike. Her confidence blossomed, and Mike noticed that she started confiding in him and telling him things that she'd previously only shared with her mom. Once he had started pouring into her through the gift of quality time, Lila saw him in a whole new light and their relationship went to another level.

Verbal Affirmations

Even if words of affirmation aren't a daughter's primary love language, they are still necessary for her to hear from her father. This is often hard for dads, whose tendency is to "show" instead of "tell" their love. But daughters, as females, are hard-wired for verbal communication, and they need to hear verbal confirmation of how their dad feels about them.

One way fathers can positively affirm their daughters is by using positive, encouraging words to build their self-esteem. Dads can try phrases like

- "I'm really proud of you for trying your best. I saw how much effort you were putting in, and that was pretty incredible."

- "You have such a creative mind! I'm impressed by all the new ideas you come up with when we're talking about things."

- "You are so strong and capable. I really believe you can do anything you make up your mind to do."

Fathers should also compliment their daughters for their efforts and their achievements, no matter how big or small. Focus on the process as much as the outcome. For instance, if a father is proud of his daughter's grade on a test, he might tell her, "I'm really proud of how well you did on that test because I know how much time you spent studying and learning the material."

Most importantly, fathers need to tell their daughters "I love you." This is especially important when they are young, because they need to know without a doubt that they are loved and cherished by their dad. When a daughter hears "I love you," she can relax and let go of any unfounded worries that she is required to earn her father's love. Instead, she can rest secure in the knowledge that her dad loves her simply because she's his daughter.

Seeking Feedback and Creating Traditions

Fathers should encourage their daughters to share what makes them feel loved and appreciated, so they can make sure to prioritize doing those things! Once the daughter has given feedback, it's also important for dads to be adaptable and willing to alter their approach based on their daughter's input.

After a daughter has shared what makes her feel most loved, her father can also use her insight to start creating traditions and rituals that will emphasize love and strengthen their connection. Remember that rituals and regular traditions don't have to be elaborate to have a big impact. I know one father who takes his daughter out for a coffee date every time she has a school delay. They sit at the coffee shop and play checkers or backgammon, and she absolutely lights up with joy every time a delay is announced because she knows it means she'll get to spend time with her dad.

There are lots of simple, easy ways that dads can create a new tradition with their daughter. Some of my favorite ideas are included below for inspiration:

- Create a special playlist of music that both dad and daughter love, and play it in the car anytime the dad is driving their daughter around so they can dance and sing together.

- Make lunch for the rest of the family on Sundays.

- Go to an age-appropriate concert or musical performance together once a year; it can be tied to a special event like a birthday or the start or end of the school year so that it happens consistently.

- Attend the first high school football game each year and split a bag of popcorn.

- Read together each night before bedtime.

- Pick out a new ornament for the Christmas tree together every year.

- Go to the county fair each year and eat the most outrageous food item you can find on the midway.

- Eat breakfast together at your favorite restaurant on the first Saturday of each month.

- Pick a new hiking trail to explore each year and hike it end-to-end together at least once during the year.

- Take a selfie together every time you do a fun dad-daughter activity.

A dad's presence means more to his daughter than either of them can fully articulate. The time that they spend together pays dividends in the daughter's future success and well-being. Conversely, a father's absence also has a profound impact on his daughter for the rest of her life. In our next chapter, we'll look more specifically at the consequences of an absent or neglectful father.

Chapter 3:

The Consequences of Absence or Neglect

> *Anyone can be a father, but it takes someone special to be a dad, and that's why I call you dad, because you are so special to me.*
> –Wade Boggs

While many daughters are lucky enough to grow up with loving, supportive dads, some daughters face the harsh reality of a father who is absent or neglectful. These experiences can leave deep scars that may eventually even affect the daughter's mental health and future relationships. In this chapter, we'll look at stories showing how daughters can be shaped by a not-so-good relationship with their father and how that experience influences their later choices. I'll also share key nuggets on the psychological impact of fatherly neglect and how its long-term impacts can create a ripple effect for the rest of the daughter's life.

How an Absent Father Affects a Daughter: A Firsthand Look

As we dive into the chapter, I'll start by walking you through three case studies of daughters who were shaped by a less-than-wonderful relationship with their fathers.

First, we'll look at the story of Ava, who faced emotional neglect from her father. While he may have been physically present, he paid about as much attention to Ava as he paid to the wallpaper. Ava's father never asked about her day, never seemed to notice if she was feeling sad or discouraged, and never showed any kind of emotion of his own in her presence.

Eventually, Ava started to believe that her feelings didn't matter and the only way to avoid feeling rejected and unwanted by her father was to become as aloof, cold, and uncaring as he appeared to be. She learned to shut off her emotions, particularly if she ever felt like they might get out of control. As a result, Ava never learned to communicate how she was feeling or express her needs and wants to the people in her life. She struggled through one unhealthy relationship after another because she assumed that it was normal for men to shut her out emotionally and fail to show any concern for her feelings or needs. It was only after Ava started seeing a therapist that she realized how emotionally closed off she'd become. With time and a lot of hard work, she finally identified and faced down the feelings of rejection she'd experienced as a child. Ava learned that it was okay to let her emotions out, and she started to hold her romantic partners to a higher standard and expect them to give her the emotional respect that she deserved.

Next, let's take a peek at Jade's story. Jade's father showed plenty of emotion; the problem was that his only emotions seemed to be anger, rage, and impatience. This often boiled over into physical violence. When he found something to get mad about, which was often, he would grab Jade by the arm and slam her against the wall or slap the back of her head so hard that she often fell down. As she grew older, Jade was smacked in the mouth any time her father felt like she was "talking back." Naturally, she became quite fearful when anyone became angry and quickly withdrew or tried to make herself invisible in tense situations.

Jade also struggled with anxiety and depression during her teenage years. She got married right after she finished college, and she did everything she could to avoid any kind of conflict with her husband. They had a hard time communicating because Jade shut down any time they disagreed about something, and her anxiety returned to such a strong degree that her husband sometimes had to take time off work to help her calm down and feel secure. The physical abuse that she'd undergone wired her brain to instantly flip into flight mode in any uncomfortable situation, and her self-esteem was almost nonexistent. Jade's husband finally convinced her to see a counselor, and while she never lost her natural aversion to conflict, Jade was able to learn some healthier coping mechanisms that reduced her anxiety levels. She gradually started to trust that disagreeing with her husband could allow them to have a healthy dialogue and wouldn't escalate into the physical violence she had experienced as a child.

Finally, let's look at Diana's story. While Diana didn't experience physical abuse, her father used words as weapons on a regular basis. Verbal abuse was common; her dad raised his voice at her daily, and the things he yelled were cruel, demeaning, and meant to tear her down. She was berated for mistakes and told that she wasn't smart enough, creative enough, attractive enough, or otherwise good enough to accomplish anything. Diana's father may not have hit her, but she was terrified of him due to his angry words. When she saw his car turn onto their street, she'd stop playing in the driveway to run inside and hide in her room, hoping to avoid his sneering criticism.

After hearing her father's verbal abuse for so long, Diana's self-esteem was completely gone, and she allowed the people around her to dictate almost everything about her life. She felt too unimportant to weigh in on even a small decision like where to go to eat when her friends wanted to have dinner at a restaurant. Then, after years of suffering from her father's verbal warfare, Diana met a friend at work who eventually shared that she had suffered verbal abuse as a child. As her friend revealed more of her story, Diana realized that it sounded a lot like how her own father had treated her. The friend introduced her to a support group and a therapist who helped Diana break out of the fog she felt like she'd been living in. Diana began to find her voice and rediscover her interests, desires, and opinions. She set strict boundaries around her communication with her father in order to create space so she could heal and rebuild her self-esteem, and she started to take back the control she'd given up so many years ago.

The Psychological Impact of Fatherly Neglect

These stories I've shared illustrate what the reality of living with fatherly abuse or neglect can look like. Next, I'd like to dive into some expert insights to help us understand the psychological underpinning of what happens to a daughter whose father neglects or abuses her.

Attachment Theory and Father-Daughter Relationships

Attachment theory is a term used to describe how a child attaches, or forms a relationship with, their parents or primary caregiver. Psychologists have generally agreed upon four different attachment styles:

- **insecure-avoidant attachment**: The child is not securely bonded to the caregiver, doesn't seem to care when the caregiver leaves, and often avoids the caregiver after they return.

- **insecure-anxious attachment**: The child is not securely bonded to the caregiver, gets very upset when the caregiver leaves, and may be anxious after the caregiver returns.

- **disorganized attachment**: The child is not securely bonded to the caregiver, their behavior fluctuates between the insecure-avoidant and insecure-anxious styles, and they often perceive the caregiver as scary or frightening.

- **secure attachment**: The child is securely bonded to the caregiver and may be momentarily upset when the caregiver leaves, but recovers quickly and is excited for the caregiver's return.

Ideally, all children would be able to form a secure attachment to both their mother and father. However, if a parent fails to meet their child's needs or harms a child instead of providing for them, an insecure or disorganized attachment will develop instead.

When a father neglects or abuses his daughter, it leads to an insecure or disorganized attachment. This has an impact far beyond childhood. How a daughter attaches to her father during her childhood influences her interactions and relationships with other people for the rest of her life. She may become anxious, clingy, and overly worried about a relationship, or conversely she may become reluctant to stand up to another person and tend to detach herself from a relationship as soon as it gets deep enough to make her uncomfortable.

Both of these extremes stem from an insecure attachment as a child, as she never learned how to create a stable, functional, supportive relationship. In fact, research has shown us that an insecure attachment to the primary caregiver can significantly decrease a person's ability to establish healthy relationships later in life (Winston & Chicot, 2016). Psychologists often call this the "father wound," a term that refers to the damaging emotional and psychological impact of a neglectful or abusive father. Whether the insecure attachment forms due to abuse, neglect, or both, a failure to attach to her father securely has long-term ramifications for a daughter.

How a Father Shapes His Daughter's Self-Worth

A secure attachment also boosts a daughter's sense of self-worth, and this is borne out by the research (Yassin, 2023). An insecure or disorganized attachment is more likely to lead to feelings of low self-worth and self-esteem. A father who's present for his daughter and treats her with kindness and respect fosters a secure attachment; his words and actions also show that he values her, which gives her a strong sense of self-worth right from the start. On the other hand, a father who's absent or who abuses his daughter creates an insecure attachment and also indirectly tells his daughter that she doesn't matter through his words and actions. This, in turn, depresses her self-esteem.

Securely attached daughters are also more likely to talk openly and often with their fathers, which boosts their mental well-being. But daughters whose fathers neglect or abuse them do not communicate with their fathers in the same way and don't experience the benefits of regular conversations with their father. A father's validation, approval, and trust has a direct impact on how his daughter views herself both during her childhood and once she becomes an adult.

Recommendations for Healing and Rebuilding Relationships

Even if a daughter has suffered abuse or neglect from her father, there is still the opportunity to find healing and hope. The first step is for the daughter to acknowledge that her relationship (or lack of relationship) with her father has caused pain. Sometimes it is very hard to acknowledge that the father has failed in some way, and daughters ignore or minimize the pain instead of accepting it for what it is.

Once the daughter has acknowledged the pain she carries as a result of her father wound, she can next identify the situations, emotions, and memories that are most likely to trigger the hurt she feels. This allows her to plan how she can cope in those situations and helps her take control of her reaction. Finally, the daughter must work to actively fight against any shame or guilt she feels in response to her woundedness. She has to love herself for who she is. Many women with a father wound are tempted to look externally and seek out another person to try to fill the void and heal their pain, but another person can never truly close up her wound. Having compassion for herself and focusing on activities that she enjoys and that nourish her are key tools to help her regain her inner strength.

Of course, this is easier said than done; while a daughter might desire healing, it often takes professional assistance to help her believe in her ability to heal. Working with a therapist, counselor, or psychologist can be a critical part of overcoming the father wound and moving past the trauma of a poor relationship with her father.

A trained professional may also be able to help the daughter identify a positive male figure so that she can see what a loving, supportive, emotionally present father looks like. Whether it's a grandfather, male relative, or family friend, a positive male role model can often play a role in her recovery and growth. Having a stable male figure can provide her with guidance and encouragement, as well as show her the qualities of a healthy relationship. This, in turn, will help her develop a better understanding of what she deserves in her own relationship and build her confidence that she is worthy of having this type of relationship.

Long-Term Effects of an Absent Father on Mental Health and Relationship Choices

Adverse experiences within the father-daughter relationship can negatively influence the daughter's mental health and relationship choices later on in life. The consequences of an abusive or neglectful situation don't end when the daughter becomes an adult and moves out on her own; they're long-term and far-reaching.

Adverse Father-Daughter Interactions and Mental Health

Anxiety and depression can stem from abuse or neglect, and statistics show that daughters whose fathers are absent or abusive are more likely to have mental health issues than daughters who have a secure relationship with their father. One study by Luo and colleagues (2011) noted a link between absent fathers and increased anxiety levels. Similarly, a 2022 study by Culpin and colleagues found that children of an absent father consistently have higher levels of depression than other children, and the correlation was particularly strong if the father was absent during their early childhood years. It's clear that when a daughter doesn't have a loving father present in her life, her mental health suffers as result.

Relationship Choices and Unhealthy Patterns

When a daughter grows up without the love and guidance of a supportive father, she may be more likely to seek out partners who do not meet her emotional needs or even subject her to the same ill treatment that she's used to receiving from her father. The absence of a positive male model can create gaps in her understanding of what a healthy, respectful relationship looks like. This can lead to settling for partners just because they're available, even if they lack the qualities necessary for a strong and fulfilling relationship, and increase the likelihood of emotional dissatisfaction and instability in the daughter's adult life.

The daughter may have a tendency to seek out validation through relationships that aren't healthy. She might also struggle with a fear of intimacy and commitment due to the trauma that she experienced in the past. After all, if her daddy can't or won't come to her aid when she needs help, who can she trust to provide a consistent, supportive presence in her life? Instead of risking more rejection, she often chooses to stay isolated and keep relationships very superficial.

That doesn't mean she has no relationships, though. Sometimes, the opposite happens: The daughter will form fleeting relationships, typically with men, that are often physically intimate but emotionally distant as she seeks out the love that she missed receiving from her father. She may use her sexuality to attract attention from men as she attempts to fill the void that her father left. These are "relationships" in name only, and they're not healthy for the daughter. Sadly, this pattern of choosing a partner based on an attempt to heal a childhood wound rather than making a healthy long-term commitment often continues to repeat itself, and the daughter continues to struggle with poor-quality relationships that further erode away at her self-esteem.

Early in the chapter, I shared the stories of three different women whose fathers were abusive or absent and the ways that their relationship with their father impacted the women even as adults. Now, I'd like to share a snapshot of a daughter who had a healthy relationship with her father to serve as a counterpoint. This woman, whom I'll call Stephanie, grew up with a dad who made the effort to spend time with her after work even if he was tired from the day. He wrestled with Stephanie when she was a small child, played basketball or baseball with Stephanie and her brother as she got a little older, and helped her build snowmen in the front lawn when it snowed. He also attended Stephanie's school events and extracurricular activities as often as he could. Stephanie's dad helped her study for tests and praised her for her hard work when she got good grades, and he was always willing to teach her how to do new things. Stephanie felt comfortable asking her dad questions, and she enjoyed hanging out with him and doing things together. When Stephanie was in college, she accepted a summer job in another state, and her dad made the 15-hour drive with her so she didn't have to drive by herself. Now that she's an adult, she and her dad still talk on the phone regularly and enjoy spending time together when they can.

Because of her good relationship with her father, Stephanie had a high standard for the men she dated. She expected to be treated with respect and consideration. She was also confident and unafraid to pursue her goals, because she'd always been told that she had the ability to achieve whatever she wanted in life. Today, Stephanie is happily married and enjoys the work she does. She's confident in her abilities, has several hobbies she's passionate about, and lives life with zest. As we move into our next chapter, I'll dive a little deeper into the ways that a loving, supportive father like Stephanie had can encourage their daughters to be independent, resilient, ambitious, and confident in everything they do.

Chapter 4:

The Role of a Father in Building Confidence

> *My mother gave me my drive, but my father gave me my dreams.*
> –Liza Minnelli

Being a young woman in today's world can be challenging, but having a supportive father can make all the difference. In this chapter, I'll walk you through the powerful role that fathers play in nurturing their daughters' confidence and independence. Fathers who encourage their daughters to take appropriate risks, help them learn from failure, and actively support their dreams and ambitions set the stage for their daughter to become a resilient adult. With the unwavering support of her father, a daughter has the foundation that she needs to thrive instead of just survive. That's because the father-daughter relationship can foster a sense of courage and determination that lasts for a lifetime.

Encouraging Independence and Resilience

Independence and resilience are essential traits for personal development. While these traits come more naturally to some girls than others, all girls have the capacity to develop them with some encouragement and support.

When a girl is independent, she can think and act for herself. She makes decisions confidently without needing to rely on others to validate her choice. Independence empowers a girl to pursue her goals and trust in her capabilities regardless of what her cheering section looks like.

Resilience means having the ability to bounce back from challenges and setbacks. Girls who have developed resilience can face challenges with a positive mindset. They learn from their experiences and keep moving forward despite the obstacles they may face.

Resilience and independence might be two slightly different qualities, but they work in tandem to build confidence. When girls feel independent, their self-esteem gets a boost, and they feel like they have control over their lives. Resilience gives them the courage to navigate life's up and downs, and along the way, they become adaptable and emotionally strong. Together, independence and resilience enhance a daughter's overall well-being and equip her to thrive no matter what life throws her way.

How Fathers Can Foster Independence

One of the best ways that fathers can encourage their daughters to develop independence is to provide them with opportunities to make decisions and solve problems. This can start from the time the daughter is very young. Dads can encourage their daughter to take the lead in small choices like picking out their clothes, deciding what kind of sandwich they want for lunch, or choosing a game to play together. These decisions might be pretty minor in the grand scheme of things, but allowing girls to make their own choices from the start gives them a sense of ownership and confidence in their ability to choose for themselves.

As she grows older, the daughter can then naturally segue into slightly more significant choices like deciding what extracurricular activities she wants to participate in or choosing her own high school classes. Along the way, she'll develop the skills she needs to make even bigger choices such as whether or not to attend college, what she wants to major in if she chooses further education, and the type of jobs she plans to pursue. Girls who started off by choosing their own clothes at age three have, over the course of their lifetime, built the confidence and critical thinking abilities necessary to feel empowered about the choices they make in their late teen years and beyond.

Fathers can also nurture independence by giving their daughters the chance to tackle challenges on their own. Instead of playing "Daddy to the rescue" and jumping in to solve every problem, dads can guide their daughters to think through the situation calmly and brainstorm possible solutions. Perhaps the daughter is struggling with a school project. Instead of doing it for her, her dad could ask questions designed to break the project down into small pieces and figure out the next step she could take. This will lead her to discover her own answers and feel confident that she can work independently on the next project.

Ultimately, fostering independence involves finding a balance between guidance and freedom. Fathers are there to teach and guide, but also to give their daughters the freedom to explore their own choices and make their own mistakes. Daughters need space to explore, play, and learn without their dad hovering over them and supervising their every move. Giving girls the space to do things on their own, whether it's mowing the lawn or walking over to a friend's house, helps them feel self-reliant. But having their father there in the background, ready to celebrate their success, helps empower a daughter to become a self-sufficient, confident, independent woman in the future.

Fathers' Role in Building Resilience

Encouraging a growth mindset is one of the foundational pieces to resilience. When a daughter has a growth mindset, she believes that she can develop her abilities and grow in intelligence through hard work, dedication, and a willingness to learn from past experiences. But a growth mindset isn't pre-programmed in children; it's something that's taught. Fathers can help their daughters adopt a growth mindset and grow in resilience by modeling this mindset themselves and making it clear that they firmly believe in growth and seeing challenges as stepping stones rather than roadblocks.

Fathers should start building resilience by affirming their daughters' efforts rather than the outcome. For instance, instead of praising a daughter for getting good grades, her father should compliment her on how hard she's been working and the effort she's been making to study and learn the material. This approach shows her that her effort matters, regardless of the outcome, and that doing her best is something to embrace.

Most importantly, dads should prioritize creating an environment where failure is viewed as a learning opportunity rather than a dead-end. Mistakes are a natural, unavoidable part of life. Thus, it's important to allow daughters to experience failure in a controlled way and to help them focus on the lessons learned instead of the failure itself. Otherwise, she'll be ill-equipped to face failure in the future and may shut down completely instead of forging ahead and trying again.

For example, if a daughter tries out for the soccer team and doesn't make it, her father could encourage her to ask the coaches what she should work on to have a better chance of making the team the next year and then spend time practicing with her and helping her improve her skills. When a father reassures his daughter that it's okay to fail and emphasizes the learning opportunity, it helps cultivate resilience.

One of the best ways to help ensure failure is viewed as an opportunity to learn is to approach challenges with curiosity. When facing difficult situations, a father can ask his daughter questions that prompt her to think critically about what went right or what went wrong and how they can improve next time. By emphasizing "next time," this encourages the resilience to try again and keep moving forward. Daughters who adopt a growth mindset and frame their struggles as a chance to learn and grow will develop the resilience they need to tackle obstacles with confidence and navigate through whatever experiences life throws their way.

The Importance of Supporting a Daughter's Ambitions

When fathers are their daughters' biggest supporter, it boosts their confidence and encourages them to pursue their ambitions. A dad's support can make or break the daughter's belief that she has the ability to chase down her dreams. When a father validates his daughter's goals by cheering her on and providing tangible assistance, she feels like she can accomplish anything she sets her mind to. Hearing a father say, through his words or his actions, "I believe in you!" sends a powerful message to his daughter that she is capable of great things.

How Fathers Can Validate Their Daughters' Ambitions

A father's validation lets his daughter know that she matters, and so do her dreams and goals. That might seem like a no-brainer, but providing a daughter with validation is one of the most important things that a father can do. Everyone needs to feel validated, and if a daughter doesn't get the support she needs from her father, she may turn to other, less healthy sources for the approval she's craving.

Providing a daughter with validation doesn't have to wait until she enters the teen years and begins questioning her place in the world. A dad can begin reassuring his daughter that she matters, that she's important, and that she's inherently good from the day she's born. A very simple way for a father to offer validation is to acknowledge her interests and passions. When a dad shows genuine interest in the things his daughter enjoys, whether that's art, music, sports, science, or something else, it encourages her to continue pursuing that passion.

Active listening and being present at her events play a huge role in acknowledging a daughter's interests. When her father listens intently and asks thoughtful questions as she chatters on about ballet, stipple painting, or the migratory habits of whales, it shows a daughter that her dad is truly present with her and considers her passions to be important simply because she thinks they're important. This validates her sense of worth by subtly letting her know that whatever she's passionate about is worthy of time and attention.

Offering encouragement during tough times is also a part of fatherly validation. A daughter may face setbacks or challenges even with activities that she enjoys, and her dad's support can give her the confidence to continue pursuing her goals. Letting the daughter know that it's okay to struggle because they can figure it out together helps her know that challenges are a part of life, but she'll always have her dad's assistance if it's needed.

Finally, a father can include his daughter in the things that he likes to do. This kind of quality builds their relationships and also helps validate her sense of self because it tells her she's worthy of her father's attention, she matters, and her company is enjoyable. In turn, she gains confidence and views herself in a positive light. The courage she has as a result helps her to go after her own goals without hesitation.

The Long-Term Impact of Fatherly Support

When fathers provide support, help their daughters become resilient and independent, and encourage them to believe their ambitions are worthwhile, it has a tangible impact. The daughter's self-esteem and confidence grow, and this leads to measurable outcomes related to long-term success.

Research has shown that daughters with supportive, involved dads are more likely to complete high school, earn a college degree, choose a higher-paying career field, overcome career challenges, and negotiate higher pay rates (Vinopal, 2019). While there are, of course, a variety of factors at play, the general consensus is that dads help instill traits that boost their daughters' empowerment, assertiveness, and sense of self-worth, which in turn encourages them to work for professional success and see it as something that's within their reach.

But success in life encompasses much more than financial and professional accomplishments, and fathers have a long-term impact in other areas, too. Social connections are a big part of our happiness, and other research suggests that fathers can influence linguistic development and the neural structures in the brain that play a role in developing trust, emotional control, and empathy (Machin, 2019). Girls who develop strong language skills and deep empathy are more likely to form strong friendships, which contribute to their overall sense of well-being.

Daughters who have a supportive father are also less likely to experience depression and other health challenges. One study found that when a father is absent from his daughter's life during her early years, she has a substantially higher likelihood of struggling with depression as an adult (Culpin et al., 2022). Physical health can be impacted by the daughter's relationship with her father, too; Nielsen (2022) indicates that having a supportive father is correlated with daughters who sleep better during childhood and develop fewer stress-related illnesses as adults.

In a nutshell, a father's support plays a role in his daughter's quality of life across her entire lifetime. From physical health to mental well-being to career success, dads who are present, involved, and encouraging give their daughters a tremendous boost in life. The reinforcement she receives as a toddler and preschooler has an exponential effect once she's a teenager, young adult, and more mature adult; what dads do during their daughters' early years can matter just as much, if not more, than what they do during their daughters' later years.

Snapshots of Success

Success can be financial, social, intellectual, and emotional, and fathers have an essential role to play in promoting success in all of these spheres. I'd like to share some snapshots of daughters whose fathers helped instill confidence in them from a young age and how the support they received from their father played a direct part in their current success.

Financial and professional success is often easiest to quantify. Jessica works in marketing and holds a VP-level position at a Fortune 100 company. Her father, who was an entrepreneur, placed a high priority on making sure his daughters had a firsthand look at his various entrepreneurial ventures and were raised with the belief that professional success could provide autonomy. Jessica's father taught her to be self-reliant and to believe that she could accomplish whatever she set out to do. She credits those early lessons as the foundation of her career success.

Jennifer's father emphasized the importance of helping others and stressed that if she had free time, she had time to assist someone in some way. That lesson resonated with Jessica, and she learned to seek out small ways that she could help someone out and make their day just a little bit better. As a result, she's built great relationships with her friends and coworkers. Her large social circle and the number of people who speak glowingly about how much better their life is due to Jennifer's presence are a testament to how her dad's influence played a direct role in her social success.

Jeannie was raised in a household that valued intellectual curiosity. Her dad managed a division of a major magazine, and his philosophy was that if someone came to him with a problem, they'd also better have a solution to offer. He taught Jeannie to think critically and take a solution-oriented approach. She was encouraged to become curious about problems and to test out possible solutions rather than giving up. Today, that same curiosity has propelled her career and helped her succeed in a variety of roles because she focuses on intellectual success and tackles every puzzle she faces head-on.

Jasmine had a strong relationship with her father, who taught her to adapt to changing circumstances, learn how to regulate her emotions, and view situations objectively instead of flying off the handle. Thanks to these early lessons, she became emotionally stable. While Jasmine doesn't live in the fanciest house on the block or drive the flashiest car in the neighborhood, she considers herself to be much happier than some of her more financially successful acquaintances because she's emotionally successful: She's able to enjoy the present moment and has fulfilling, secure relationships. The internal sense of self-worth that her father cultivated in her, along with the lessons on emotional maturity, have played a big role in her happiness and emotional success.

While each of these women have found success in different ways, one of the common denominators is their relationship with their father and the values he instilled in them from a young age. In all cases, their dads were present in their lives and formed an intentional relationship with their daughter. Each father also identified the trait or characteristics that they felt were essential to success, and they worked hard to make sure their daughters felt both competent and confident in this area.

Another related note in these women's stories is relationships. Their dads helped them build skills that set them up for strong future relationships, whether that was due to having a passion for helping others, a desire to help others solve problems, or being mature and emotionally stable. Fathers shape their daughters' future relationships in myriad ways, and in our next chapter we'll turn our attention to a dad's role in helping his daughter form healthy relationships later in her life.

Chapter 5:

How Good Dads Shape Healthy Relationships

Daddies don't just love their children every now and then, it's a love without end.
—George Strait

A daughter might live under her dad's roof only for the first 18 or so years of her life, but his influence will be felt long after she moves out on her own. One of the major ways this happens is through her father's impact on her choice of a romantic partner. At first, this might be a head-scratcher; after all, the daughter chooses her own partner, so how does her father play a role? What you'll come to understand by the end of this chapter is that dads play a huge part in laying the foundation for what a daughter will expect from her future romantic partner and her perception of what a healthy relationship looks like. She may choose her own partner, but underlying her choice is an unconscious set of beliefs that were shaped long before she even started dating.

Since dads play such an outsized, if unseen, role in their daughters' future relationships, it's very important for them to teach their daughters how to establish a respectful foundation and set healthy boundaries. The way a father treats his daughter and his daughter's mom has a ripple effect that extends out into his daughter's life for many years.

A Father's Influence on His Daughter's Partner

The father-daughter relationship has a key role to play in helping shape how the daughter sees herself. This, in turn, has a direct impact on how she views her relationships. The way her dad communicates, behaves, and shows support sets the tone for the daughter's future expectations in her relationships, starting with her friendships and moving into her romantic partnerships.

Father-Daughter Interactions, Emotional Foundations, and Relationship Expectations

From a young age, a father's engagement with his daughter really shapes how the daughter views herself and the expectations she has for her future relationships. We looked at how fathers can build trust with their daughters in Chapter 1, and this actually has repercussions for the daughter's relationships, too. Daughters who feel secure and valued by their dad are more likely to trust easily in their future relationships. They haven't put up walls or shut off their heart because they've always been able to rely on their dad, and they have the subconscious expectation that they'll be able to rely on their partner, too.

In fact, research has shown that when a father makes his daughter feel valued, it creates a tremendous sense of security in her future relationships (Roberts, 2020). She sees those relationships as a partnership based on mutual benefit, versus searching for the attention that she never received as a child. Dads lay this foundation from a young age, even as early as age two, so fathers should understand that it's never too soon to start setting the groundwork for how their daughter should be treated by her future romantic partners.

A father doesn't have to rely on grand, extravagant gestures to build this trust, either. Simple, routine interactions like reading bedtime stories, playing board games, or taking walks together all send a strong message to the daughter: "You are valued, and you are worthy of my time." As a result, she will expect the people she forms relationships with in the future to value her as well. She'll think of herself as worthy of their time and attention, because that's the standard her father set for her.

Additionally, father-daughter interactions play a role in the daughter's emotional intelligence. This, in turn, directly influences how she relates to and interacts with people in future relationships. A father plays a huge role in helping his daughter understand that it's okay to experience and communicate emotions. If he comforts her when she's feeling sad, upset, scared, or anxious and lets her know that it's okay to experience big feelings, she learns that she can safely be open about how she feels to the people she's closest with. On the other hand, if her father dismisses her emotions or shuts them down, the daughter learns that she cannot trust other people with her emotions and may have a hard time being emotionally vulnerable with others in the future.

Fathers and the Standard They Set

Early interactions between a father and his daughter lay the groundwork for how the daughter will perceive her future relationships, and this has been borne out by the research (Hall, 2009). Positive, supportive, and engaged fatherhood helps girls grow into confident, emotionally intelligent women who value healthy and fulfilling connections with others. Fathers truly do set the standard for how their daughters should expect to be treated by others as they move into adulthood.

Fathers set this standard both by how they treat their daughter, and by how they treat others. We've looked at some of the ways that fathers can influence their daughters' self-esteem, confidence, and self-reliance, and all of those factors contribute to their future relationship choices. Furthermore, daughters learn what a relationship looks like by watching their father. When he treats others with kindness, compassion, and respect, she learns that this is what an adult relationship looks like and will seek out similar relationships. However, if a father is demeaning, belittles others, or creates an unreasonable standard in his relationships, then his daughter will learn that this is a "normal" way of treating others and is more likely to accept being treated this way in the future.

Another way that fathers set the standard for their daughters' future relationships is in the type and frequency of their communication. When a father communicates openly and respectfully with his daughter, he sets a standard for how communication occurs in a relationship. Talking with his daughter regularly, showing interest in the events of her day, and asking about her friends and activities all model healthy communication to her. The way a dad handles disagreements is also important. When he models how to disagree calmly and respectfully, he teaches his daughter how to resolve relationship conflict in a positive manner. She'll likely look for a romantic partner who shows a similar interest in her life and is also willing to handle conflict with respect.

It's important for fathers to be as consistent as possible with the standards they set. If a father fluctuates between being loving and respectful at one moment and harsh and judgmental the next, it can create a lot of confusion for the daughter. She may consequently struggle to understand what kind of behavior is typical in relationships and, later in life, be drawn to partners who are similarly inconsistent, which can lead to unstable relationships.

For better or worse, a father's behavior serves as a roadmap for his daughter. It shapes her expectations for her future relationships. By modeling positive treatment and respect, fathers can empower their daughters to seek out healthy, loving partnerships. Conversely, the opposite is true: Dads who model negative behaviors can influence their daughters toward an unhealthy dynamic in future relationships. Fathers have a key role to play, so it's important for them to be mindful of how they relate to both their daughter and to others.

Psychologist Jennifer Kromberg (2013) has noted that, across many years of practice, she's had very few female patients whose adult relationships did not in some way reflect their relationship with their father. Even if a daughter actively chooses a romantic partner who completely contrasts with their father, he's still impacted her choice. Some women, due to a negative relationship with their father, might intentionally seek out someone who is the opposite of their father in many ways. They've learned from their father what they do *not* want their partner to be like, and they aren't afraid of their father's disapproval if he's upset that they have chosen to form a relationship with someone who is so different.

Other women who have a strong relationship with their father might subconsciously seek out someone who resembles their father not just because of the positive standard that he set, but because they want to receive their father's approval of their relationship. They value their dad's opinion, and that means they also value their dad's opinion of their partner.

Fatherly Examples and Preventing Abusive Relationships

As we've discussed, a strong father makes a significant difference in his daughter's life by helping her understand what healthy relationships look like. Next, we'll explore how fathers play a crucial role in teaching their daughters about respect, communication, and setting healthy boundaries—thus equipping their daughters with information and skills to help avoid abusive relationships in the future.

Fathers who treat their partners with kindness and respect reinforce the idea that a healthy relationship is built on mutual service. Showing compassion and affection for their partner actually helps their daughter feel more secure, in addition to giving her a strong example for the future. For instance, when a dad helps with chores or volunteers to drive the carpool on a particularly busy morning, his daughter sees firsthand that love and respect are crucial for building a strong partnership. Conversely, if a father repeatedly practices negative behaviors like interrupting or talking to his partner in a dismissive, rude, or condescending manner, his daughter might interpret those behaviors as normal and acceptable in a relationship.

Fathers who model positive behavior in their own relationships set a powerful standard for their daughters, and fathers who educate their daughters on recognizing red flags that may signal an unhealthy or abusive relationship, empower their daughters to be proactive about their well-being. This gives their daughter a leg up in avoiding harmful situations, as well as equipping them with the confidence to leave relationships where they are not respected or valued.

What Dads Teach Their Daughters About Boundaries and Respect

Dads have a vital role to play in teaching their daughter about respect, boundaries, and communication. One of the first lessons in respect comes from how the father treats his daughter. For example, asking what she thinks and listening to her opinions tells the daughter that her voice matters and it's important for her to be heard. A father who takes the time to slow down and listen to his daughter, rather than ignore her or steamroll over her ideas, encourages her to demand the same level of respect in her future relationships.

When a father respects personal boundaries—both his daughter's and others'—it teaches his daughter the importance of healthy boundaries. By demonstrating with his words and actions that everyone deserves their own space and the ability to make their own decisions, his daughter will be more likely to seek out a partner who also respects her boundaries and autonomy. Fathers can also model what it looks like to set boundaries. Even things like establishing rules at home about screen time or family dinners, to give a couple of examples, will help his daughter understand that boundaries are essential for maintaining healthy relationships.

Furthermore, when a dad encourages his daughter to speak up when someone oversteps boundaries—whether that's a friend being too pushy or a date who spends most of dinner on his phone—he is teaching her to stand up for herself and set limits in her relationships. She's learned, from her dad, that it's okay to have expectations for how she should be treated and to call out when others are not living up to those expectations.

Communication is a big part of helping a daughter learn to expect that others will treat her respectfully and honor her boundaries. When dads are closed off about their emotions and experiences, it can feel like they are simply giving orders and imparting expectations without any true, back-and-forth communication. This, in turn, teaches their daughter that relationships are more about rules and tasks than reciprocal interaction. However, dads who are open about their feelings and willing to express their emotions teach their daughters how important it is to share emotions.

For instance, a dad who comes home from work and shares that he's feeling tired and overwhelmed, as well as letting his daughter know that he's going for a walk around the block to decompress, shows her how to find healthy ways to cope with stress and let out negative feelings. When she grows up, she'll then be more likely to openly communicate her emotions and needs to her partner as well as encourage them to do the same.

From an early age, the way a father interacts with his daughter will set the tone for what she expects in her future relationships. By modeling healthy behaviors, including respectful communication, a dad provides the example that will shape his daughter's perception of what a healthy partnership looks like. In turn, this equips her to build strong, respectful relationships that avoids an unhealthy dynamic.

Recognizing Red Flags and the Need to Maintain Independence

It's important for dads to teach their daughters to recognize red flags that might indicate an abusive or unhealthy relationship, as well as ways to protect themselves and make informed choices. The reality is that many daughters may not be aware of what unhealthy behaviors look like, especially as they're first starting to form and navigate romantic relationships during their teenage years. Furthermore, any familial trauma or harmful relationships in the daughter's own family may have desensitized them to red flags in a relationship. As Teri Clark (2021) put it, "Kids and adults learn what they live and that includes harmful relationships," which is another reminder of how important it is for dads to make sure their own relationships are respectful and positive.

One way that dads can teach their daughters about unhealthy relationship behaviors is to discuss real-life scenarios or behaviors. For instance, a daughter might feel excited when the cute boy in her math class wants to spend all of their time together. But her dad can make sure she knows that if he tries to isolate her from her family or friends, attempts to control her time, or gets angry when she spends time with anyone else, it's a sign that the relationship has crossed a line and is no longer healthy.

Fathers can also make sure their daughters know the difference between appropriate and inappropriate communication. It's important for a dad to teach his daughter that a partner who reacts with anger or tries to intimidate her instead of discussing concerns calmly is a big red flag. Healthy relationships are build on open dialogue, not name-calling or threats, and that's a lesson that dads can impart to their daughters.

In addition to helping their daughters identify potential red flags, dads can provide the support their daughters need to leave a relationship that's potentially harmful. Fathers who build a relationship where their daughters feel comfortable speaking to them openly create an avenue for their daughter to seek out advice if she feels uncertain or unsafe. She'll know that her dad will always have her back and offer the soft landing she needs to leave a potentially negative situation.

One of the biggest ways that a dad can help his daughter avoid an abusive or unsafe relationship is teaching her independence. A girl who has the educational background to maintain financial independence opens up options for herself, and she won't have to stay in a negative relationship simply because she's dependent on her partner. In our next chapter, we'll talk in detail about how fathers can promote independence in their daughter to help protect them against a bad situation.

Real-Life Relationships: Showcasing a Father's Gift

My good friend Sheila was blessed to have a great relationship with her dad. He attended all her dance recitals, took her out for pie at the local diner on snow days, and made her pancakes on Saturday mornings. They loved talking about their favorite movies and frequently quoted movies to each other during conversations. Sheila's dad also treated her mom with respect and kindness, taking her out on regular date nights and spending time together talking and laughing.

When Sheila was in high school, she started dating a guy named Benji. He was charismatic and funny, and she quickly started spending more and more time with him. Benji gradually convinced Sheila to start skipping classes and drop out of her extracurricular activities to hang out with him. He also started attacking her self-esteem and made her feel like he was always on the verge of breaking off their relationship, so she needed to work a little harder. Sheila started losing weight and withdrawing from her other friends and family members.

Her dad noticed the change in his daughter, and one Saturday he made her some special smiley-face pancakes and asked her quite bluntly what was going on in her life and if Benji had anything to do with the changes. Sheila was hesitant at first, but eventually confessed that she'd been skipping class to hang out with Benji so that he didn't break up with her. She told her dad some of the things Benji had been saying to her, and how overwhelmed she was starting to feel by the relationship.

Sheila's dad listened to her quietly. When she was finished, he made her some hot chocolate. Then he sat down, looked her in the eye, and told her that if a boy was using the threat of breaking up as a way to keep her in the relationship, it sounded to him like a relationship that wasn't too healthy to begin with. He reminded Sheila that relationships are supposed to be built on kindness, trust, and respect and asked her if Benji exhibited those qualities. She started crying, and her dad just hugged her. Then, he asked her if she wanted to call Benji and break it off. He held her hand while she made the phone call and then put on her favorite movie.

Every day for the next week, Sheila's dad came home with flowers: one bouquet for her mom, and one bouquet for Sheila. The last bouquet had a note for Sheila, reminding her that a guy worthy of her time and attention wouldn't call her names. He would bring her flowers. Sheila still has the note to this day, and she ended up marrying a man who did, in fact, bring her flowers.

Chapter 6:

Raising Independent Daughters

> *When a father gives his daughter an emotional visa to strike out on her own, he is always with her. Such a daughter has her encouraging, understanding daddy in her head, cheering her on—not simply as a woman but as a whole, unique human being with unlimited possibilities.*
> –Victoria Secunda

One of the best ways a father can help his daughter make good choices for the future is raising her to be independent: emotionally, educationally, and financially. A daughter who's independent is, as we discussed in Chapter 4, able to rely on herself. She is less likely to be trapped in a bad relationship with no way of getting out, and she'll have the skills to handle life's transitions with grace and confidence. Specifically, we'll also look at how education plays a key role in empowering a daughter to be financially independent.

The Importance of Financial Independence

Some fathers may wonder why I place so much emphasis on financial importance, or what's wrong with having a daughter who depends on her significant other to take care of some if not all of their financial needs. While there's certainly nothing wrong with sharing finances and even having one partner contribute more to their cash flow than the other, what I'd like to stress is how important it is for women to have the knowledge and skills to support themselves financially if necessary. That includes the ability to earn a living wage as well as some basic financial literacy skills to manage their money intelligently.

What financial independence provides for daughters is a voice. She'll never be completely dependent on her partner and forced to live by their rules, whether healthy or not, if she knows she can go out and earn her own way. In fact, financial independence once protected my cousin from a potentially abusive relationship. She had moved in with her boyfriend and he'd talked her into combining their finances into a joint bank account and cutting her hours down to part-time because he was going to take care of things. He slowly started to turn the "joint" account into "his" account, even going so far as to tell my cousin that he'd cancelled her debit card and would give her a weekly allowance in cash instead.

She got a bad feeling and let him know that she was going to move out and end the relationship. He began making threats at that point, telling her that he was going to freeze the account, and she wouldn't be able to pay rent unless she stayed with him. But since my uncle had taught my cousin some basic financial literacy, she was able to open her own account and start managing her own money again. She also went back to work on a full-time basis and was able to cover her rent easily. Luckily, the workplace skills and financial know-how that she'd learned in her teen years allowed her to break things off with the boyfriend before the situation escalated and she was in a situation that could have gotten seriously dangerous.

Imparting Basic Financial Literacy

It's important for fathers to teach their daughters some basic financial concepts. That includes budgeting and saving, but also extends into topics like bank accounts, credit cards, and investments. Dads who talk with their daughters about these concepts early on—and give them the opportunity to practice when the stakes are low—set their daughters up for financial success later in life. They'll know how to manage their money, what it means to spend wisely, and how important it is to create a financial cushion by contributing to a savings account and planning for the future.

I want to emphasize here that money isn't inherently good or bad; it's a tool, and like all tools, it should be used wisely. That's where fathers come in. Even the language that a father uses to talk about finances with his daughter is important. A father who has a negative relationship with money will subconsciously pass that along to his daughter and vice versa.

Even when a daughter is very young, playing games like Life or Monopoly will help introduce her to managing finances and how spending or saving money can affect things later on. As a bonus, time spent playing board games together strengthens the father-daughter relationship in other ways!

Dads can also make sure they talk about finances and the choices they're making in front of their daughters in order to model positive behavior. For instance, a dad might mention out loud that he's been saving part of his paycheck every month to set aside for their family vacation later in the year, or talk about how he just paid off his credit card in advance of the payment deadline to avoid incurring high interest. Taking a daughter to the store while doing errands is another great way to expose her to the idea that things cost money, and that it's important to be a smart consumer and think about wants versus needs when making purchases.

As a daughter gets older, giving her an allowance gives her a chance to practice managing her own money on a very limited basis, when the stakes are still quite low. Some parents may decide to gradually increase the daughter's allowance as she gets older but also task her with the responsibility of paying for most if not all of her own expenses.

In fact, I have one good friend whose father opened a checking account for her on her thirteenth birthday. From that point forward, he put a set amount of money in the account at the start of each month, and she was responsible for budgeting her spending for the month accordingly. Her dad paid her car insurance when she started driving and her cell phone bill once she got a cell phone, but all other expenses—her clothes, eating out with friends, tickets to the movies, school supplies, gas for her car, and the like—were on her, using the money that was deposited in her account each month. If she blew everything during a start-of-month shopping spree, she was out of luck when her friends made plans to go out to eat later in the month.

To this day, she credits her dad for helping her learn how to budget and plan her spending at a time when the consequences were fairly low.

If she ran out of money, the worst that happened was that she had to say no when her friends wanted to go do something. It was painful at the time, but much less painful than deciding between paying the electric bill or buying groceries as an adult.

Teaching a daughter to budget is incredibly important, but financial literacy doesn't stop there. Dads should also talk with their daughters about savings accounts and the value of saving money for future purchases as well as for even more long-term goals like retirement. Suggesting to the daughter that she set aside a certain percentage of her allowance is a great start, as is encouraging her to get a part-time job when she's a teenager and to put part of her paycheck into savings.

Dads may even want to consider incentivizing their daughter to set financial goals and start saving money. My friend whose dad taught her to budget by putting her in charge of all her expenses learned to save from her dad, too. He told her, starting around age 10, that he would match her savings (up to $5,000) when she was ready to buy her first car. She did some babysitting, had a part-time job, and made sure to put part of her monthly allowance into her savings account, and her dad was true to his word. She had accumulated a little over $3,000 by the time she got her driver's license, and he matched that amount when she started car-shopping. She had some incentive to save, and she also learned what it meant to contribute to a savings account thanks to her dad.

Finally, fathers should remember that financial literacy also includes teaching their daughters some fundamental principles when it comes to credit cards, debt, and investing. Sadly, many girls get into trouble as young adults because they don't fully realize the implications of carrying credit card debt and how quickly the interest can pile up. The implications extend even further as their credit score declines, hurting their ability to qualify for things like a home loan in the future. A dad can give his daughter a leg up by making sure she's aware how to use credit responsibly and why having good credit is important.

Daughters also need to know the difference between saving and investing. Teaching a daughter to put money in her savings account is a great start, but talking to her about setting aside some of her savings to invest for the future will help boost her to become truly financially literate. A dad could help his daughter put some of her money into a short-term certificate of deposit (CD) instead of a savings account so she can see firsthand how investing can pay off dividends in the future. He can also make sure she hears him talking about the investments he's made, whether that is contributing to a 401k through his employer or owning some shares of a few stocks.

If a father feels uncomfortable or unqualified to talk with his daughter about finances, it actually creates a great opportunity for them to learn together. Seeing her dad admit that he needs to understand things a little better himself signals to the daughter that it's okay to admit when you don't know something and need to educate yourself further. It also cues her in to how important it is to be a lifelong learner. Plus, the time they spend learning together—whether that's through books, webinars, or meeting with a financial advisor in person—can be a wonderful bonding experience.

Education as a Means to Independence

While it's certainly possible to become financially independent without any education, there's also no doubt that an education very often plays a huge role in a daughter's finances. I want to make clear here that in speaking about the importance of education, I'm not referring to strictly a college education. Finishing high school is important, and trade schools, vocational training, or apprenticeship programs are all excellent options for girls who know they want to pursue a career path that doesn't necessarily require a college degree. The point is that giving a girl training and a skillset equips her for a job that subsequently allows her to earn an income without being reliant upon someone else to pay her bills.

A dad can help lay the groundwork for his daughter's later education even before she is old enough to go to school. Reading to her and engaging in interactive play has been shown to translate to better academic performance at ages five and seven (Kiderlin, 2023). Another way fathers help their daughter succeed in school is by encouraging her to work hard in the classroom from an early age. Fathers should praise their daughters for their effort, not necessarily for the results. Different academic subjects come more easily to some girls than to others, and what fathers want their daughters to internalize is that hard work pays off. Instead of saying, "Great job, honey. I'm really proud of you for acing that test!" a dad can say, "Great job, honey. I'm really proud of how hard you studied to prepare for that test!"

When a father shows interest in his daughter's academic work, asks her questions about school, and recognizes her efforts, it creates a higher level of confidence that translates into greater academic success. Suizzo and colleagues (2016) found a correlation between fathers' attitude toward their daughter's schoolwork and the daughter's optimism about her ability to succeed in school, and fathers' involvement has also been shown to reduce truancy rates (Jeynes, 2018). Even if the daughter decides not to pursue additional education, finishing her high school degree is tremendously valuable in terms of her work opportunities.

For girls who do plan to continue their education after high school, dads play an important role in helping them explore diverse career paths. Spending time with his daughter and talking to her about the type of work he does may help open her eyes to career fields that have historically been considered masculine, like math, engineering, or construction. Some research has found that women born within the last 50 years are three times more likely to work in the same field as their father than women born 100 years ago, indicating that as daughters receive more mentoring from their fathers, they're also more likely to follow in his career footsteps (Nielsen, 2014).

Fathers can also be a big influence when their daughter is deciding what type of education, if any, to pursue after high school. Dads can and should accompany their daughters on college visits, if she is interested in higher education. They can also help look into alternative education options such as trade schools and apprenticeship programs. Talking with a daughter about her interests and career goals helps her feel confident about her choices and also gives her father a better understanding of the training she might need to pursue and the options she may want to look into.

It's important for dads to remember that while a collegiate education is necessary for many career fields, it also isn't the "be-all end-all" if a daughter's interests lay elsewhere. I have two friends who are both cosmetologists. One of them attended a cosmetology training program and, within a year, was a licensed cosmetologist working in a salon. The other knew that she wanted to go into cosmetology but was pushed into attending a four-year university by her dad. Four years and thousands of dollars in debt later, she worked briefly in an office before leaving to attend a cosmetology school and pursue her passion.

My friend who went directly to a training program is now a salon owner, as she was able to pay off her cosmetology program in just a few months and then set aside her savings toward opening her own place. My other friend who first attended college is still paying off her student loans and puts most of her savings toward her student debt. When a dad truly listens to his daughter and encourages her to pursue the education and training that make the most sense for the goals that *she* has in life, he plays a powerful role in supporting the decisions that will have the greatest benefit for her future.

Teaching Daughters to Value Themselves

As we've discussed in previous chapters, dads have a crucial role to play in boosting their daughters' self-esteem and confidence. A healthy self-esteem and high confidence levels, in turn, can open many doors in the future. One long-term study showed a strong correlation between teenagers' self-esteem and their future career success, clearly indicating that dads who help their daughters build healthy self-esteem are actually boosting their long-term success, too (Blouin, 2022).

A Father's Role in Helping His Daughter Appreciate Her Strengths

A father is uniquely positioned to recognized his daughter's strengths and appreciate what makes her unique. After all, he's known her since birth and watched her learn and grow over the years! That means a father also has a singular opportunity to encourage his daughter to choose a career path that fits her talents.

Girls might not always recognize their own strengths, so their dad's input can make more of a difference than he realizes. For instance, if a girl is naturally gifted in math, it might not seem like that big of a deal because it comes so easily to her. But if her dad mentions to her that he's noticed how quickly she picks up math concepts and encourages her to keep developing her gift for numbers, that will help her realize that math is actually an area of strength for her.

Dads can also provide opportunities for their daughters to keep growing their strengths, whether that's by signing them up for a soccer team, enrolling them in art classes, or taking them to the library and picking out some books about the topic together. By doing these things, a father subtly tells his daughter that she should continue to develop her gifts to see where that leads her. She may end up developing a lifelong passion or discovering her career goal!

Once a daughter is ready to set some long-term goals, her dad can and should be her greatest supporter. Together, they can create a plan for reaching her goals and map out the major steps or actions she'll need to take to accomplish them. A father can then check in regularly to remind his daughter of her goals and motivate her to stay focused.

Helping Daughters Prepare for Life Transitions

Life transitions are inevitable: moving out of their parents' house into their own apartment, starting a first job, getting married, having children—daughters will experience many potential "firsts" after they leave childhood behind. A father can serve as a guiding light through many of these major transitions, but his most valuable role might be laying the groundwork that teaches essential skills and prepares his daughter to tackle challenges independently.

Sadly, there is evidence showing that fewer and fewer teens are prepared to transition independently into adulthood because their parents have never allowed them to start taking responsibility and making decisions (Carroll, 2024). However, the evidence also indicates that fathers are uniquely equipped to help their children prepare to transition into independent adulthood (Carroll, 2024). When a father does his job well, his daughter has learned to make informed decisions without completely relying on her parents for help. She's ready for the responsibilities of adulthood.

One of the best ways that dads can help their daughters prepare for life transitions is to help them get ready in advance. Fathers can help their daughters mentally "rehearse" their way through the transition. For instance, if a daughter is getting ready to move into her first apartment, her dad can talk her through the steps she'll need to take—from unpacking to setting up utilities to paying the rent on time. Daughters may sometimes feel shy or hesitant about admitting what they don't know, so fathers can foster an environment where questions are welcomed and answers are thoughtful and helpful.

Teaching a daughter to problem-solve is valuable not just for helping them through transitions, but also for preparing them to be independent. While daughters are young, dads can help them start learning to problem-solve by being a role model and articulating their own problem-solving strategies out loud. Whether that's fixing something broken, figuring out how to handle a delicate situation, or setting up the weekly carpool, a father can verbalize his thought process and talk about the pros and cons of various options before making a decision. This gives his daughter a firsthand glimpse of what it looks like to solve a problem.

Helping a daughter identify and recognize a small problem before it snowballs into something much larger is also an invaluable skill for a dad to impart to her. It will be much easier for her to independently troubleshoot a minor issue than waiting until it turns into something major that might require a lot more help and resources to tackle. Plus, when a daughter is able to spot and preemptively fix a small problem, it gives her confidence in her abilities and the knowledge that she's prepared to live independently.

From fostering financial independence to encouraging education and placing a high value on her abilities, dads play a key role in helping their daughters become independent adults. Consistency is a big part of doing so, because forming good financial and educational habits is a process rather than a one-time event. In our next chapter, we'll look more deeply into the value of consistency and why it's so important for dads to be a reliable presence in their daughters' lives.

Chapter 7:

The Quiet Strength of Consistency

Dads are most ordinary men turned into heroes, adventurers, storytellers and singers of song.
–Pam Brown

Fathers are a critical presence in their daughters' lives, and establishing a routine is one of the best ways that a dad can create a sense of security, value, and support for his daughter. From being consistently available to sharing activities and communicating regularly, a dad who is constantly present creates a stable father-daughter relationship.

A Consistent Presence Builds Lasting Security

When a dad proves to his daughter that he's reliable—he is present when he says he'll be present, and he follows through on his promises—it builds a strong sense of trust. His daughter knows that she can rely on her dad, and she never questions whether he'll be there for her if she needs him.

It's important for a dad to start creating this sense of security from the time his daughter is very young. Trust is easier to establish from the start; a father proving to his daughter that he's trustworthy after years of unreliability is much more difficult. Dads should also remember that children experience time differently than adults. Waiting 10 minutes for her dad to finish up a project before they play a game can feel like a lifetime to a young daughter! So being present and available when a father says he will, instead of 10 or 15 minutes later, makes a big difference to a daughter.

When a dad can set aside specific times each week to eat dinner with his daughter, help her with homework, or share a special activity, he shows his daughter that he is dependable. In turn, she understands that she's a priority in her father's life.

For a daughter, feeling like a priority and understanding that her father values her has a big impact on her self-esteem. She'll grow up feeling worthy of attention and secure in the knowledge that her dad sees her, so she will be less likely to act out or behave recklessly as a cry for attention. She'll also be more confident, because she won't constantly be questioning if there is something "wrong" with her that makes her dad ignore her or put her at the bottom of his priority list. The research bears this out; one study found that daughters who had a close relationship with their fathers had higher self-esteem during adolescence (Bohn, 2021).

Measurable Outcomes Due to Consistency

In fact, a consistent, persistent relationship between a father and his daughter has been shown to produce better outcomes when the daughter is an adult. Emotional intelligence is higher in daughters whose dads regularly engaged with them emotionally during their childhood, for instance (*Father Daughter Relationships*, 2024).

A study by Flouri and Buchanan (2003) found that girls whose father was heavily involved in their life during childhood were better psychologically adjusted as adults and were less likely to experience psychological distress in their 30s. Haaz and colleagues (2014) conducted research that indicated women who had a strong relationship with their fathers also reported higher levels of intimacy in their marriage, indicating that their bond with their father influenced their relationships later in life.

The National Fatherhood Initiative, an organization that seeks to increase fathers' involvement by support initiatives that are pro-father, has collected a wide range of research on fathers and the impact they have on their children. Their evidence has pointed to many benefits of involved fathers, including the following (*Statistics Tell the Story*, n.d.):

- When a father regularly plays with his infant daughter, she has higher mental and social outcomes later in life.

- Fathers who read to their daughters on a regular basis help them develop better thinking and language skills.

- Daughters whose dads are a consistent part of their life have fewer behavior problems in middle school and lower levels of stress and depression as teenagers.

- Social and emotional well-being are positively influenced when dads are highly involved in their daughters' life.

- Girls whose fathers are a consistent presence in their life are less likely to have children outside of a stable relationship and are less likely to raise their children alone.

- A father's consistent presence has been linked to lower rates of infant mortality, obesity, poor performance in school, injuries, teen pregnancy, criminal activity, abusing alcohol and drugs, and suicide.

The statistics are clear: A dad who's regularly present and who is intentionally active in his daughter's life lays a foundation for her future success in a myriad of ways. From her relationships to her career to her mental health, her dad's involvement in her life as a child has a huge impact.

The Role of Routine in Stable Relationships

Having a routine has demonstrated psychological benefits. From infants to adults, we all thrive with a consistent, predictable schedule. Routines can help us eat better, sleep better, handle stress better, and stay more active.

This is all due to the fact that routines relieve us of many minor decisions, and each decision we have to make causes some level of stress. If we don't have a routine and have to decide on a daily basis when to get up, when to get dressed, when to brush our teeth, what time to leave the house, and so on, all of those small decisions cause stress to start adding up. However, a morning routine means most of those decisions have been made for us; we simply get up at the same time each day and follow our morning routine of getting dressed, brushing teeth, and leaving at a specific time. It's extremely low-stress because we're allowing the routine to make the choices for us.

Routines also help us spend more time with our loved ones and free us up to participate in activities we enjoy. When our regular daily tasks are captured within a routine, we can move through them quickly and automatically, and we know when we'll be finished with the routine and available for leisure activities. We can also intentionally plan our routines to include more time with family and other loved ones, such as a regular family dinner or a standing get-together with a friend group.

Fathers can harness the power of routine to help them relate to their daughters better. A consistent, predictable routine helps dads carve out time to spend with their daughters and gives their daughters peace of mind in knowing when their dads will be around.

Creating a Consistent, Predictable Routine

To create a strong routine that helps bond fathers and daughters, it's important to remember that routines don't have to be complicated or time-consuming to be effective. Something as simple as listening to a particular playlist on the drive home from practice or getting donuts together on Sunday mornings still counts as a relationship-building routine!

Everyone's time is limited, and prioritizing quality time over quantity time is a great way for dads to take advantage of the time they have and maximize their father-daughter interactions. When a father and daughter have a small number of things that they consistently do together, that can be just as powerful (or even more so) as a father and daughter who are physically together often but rarely intentionally connect during that time. Coming up with a few ideas of things to do together and then committing to them will have major benefits for the relationship and will ensure the daughter feels loved, valued, and important.

Some routines might revolve around something very consistent and practical, like doing errands together on Saturdays, raking leaves together every fall, or carrying the garbage out together on trash night. Other routines might be purely for fun, like dance parties, while many routines combine a practical task with a fun twist.

To help fathers get started thinking about some routines they might want to implement with their daughters, I've compiled a list of ideas. These are meant to serve as a jumping-off point; they can and should be modified in any way necessary to best meet the needs of a particular father and daughter, and this certainly is not an all-inclusive list! Some of the many activities fathers and daughters could incorporate into their own routine for spending time together include

- playing a card game or board game on a specific night of the week

- having tea parties on Sunday afternoons

- setting a standing lunch date for the first Monday (or Tuesday, or Wednesday...) of each month

- taking a selfie together on the first or last day of each month

- working out together two to three times a week

- going to a minor league baseball game, collegiate basketball game, or other sporting event each season

- having a dance party after dinner while doing the dishes

- volunteering for a local charity on a monthly or bimonthly basis

- getting ice cream together after sports practice

- going kayaking or fishing together on every family vacation

- getting pedicures together before the start of each school year (Dads can get a masculine version that doesn't involve nail polish!)

- building a fort out of couch cushions each weekend and then watching a movie from inside the fort

- picking a new recipe to cook together once a month

- creating a secret handshake or secret greeting

- dressing up and going out on a fancy dinner date for each of their birthdays

- bathing the family dog together and having a contest to see who can stay the driest; the winner gets to pick a dessert to share

- going to a concert together once a year

- building a new Lego set together monthly

- finding an interesting science experiment online and doing it together each time she brings home a report card (regardless of the grades on the card)

- shoveling the driveway and making a snowman every year during the first snowfall and then going inside for hot chocolate

- writing a letter to the daughter every year on her birthday

- dancing in the rain together every spring

- going outside to look at the night sky when the moon is full

- fighting a water balloon battle on the Fourth of July

- visiting the library together once a week and picking out books for each other

- exploring a local or state park and hiking the trails monthly

- looking at the school lunch menu for the week together to plan out packing days and buying days

- playing games together during car rides, like the alphabet game or "I Spy"

Many of these routines can be practiced weekly or monthly. Other rituals involve celebrating specific annual milestones or happenings. While this type of routine might not be as front-and-center as a weekly routine, the rituals tied to life events can be just as important. They show a daughter that her growth is important and her efforts matter, and that her dad recognizes the importance of the milestone.

It's also important to remember to remain flexible. Life can be unpredictable, and routines may need to adapt to accommodate changes. Sometimes that means a Saturday morning activity has to get skipped for a week or take place on a different day because the family has other plans, and sometimes that means the routine itself changes as the daughter grows older. For example, a dad might start a ritual of having a tea party with his young daughter on Sunday afternoons. As she gets older, the tea party may no longer hold her interest and their routine could change to involve Legos or practicing soccer in the backyard on Sundays instead. Or, a dad and his daughter might have a Saturday morning ritual of running errands and getting donuts—until she joins a volleyball team that practices on Saturday mornings, meaning that their new routine is singing in the car on the way to practice and getting smoothies on the way home.

Flexibility and adaptability allow routines to change as the daughter's needs change; it also keeps the relationship strong because it shows the daughter that their bond is more important than any scheduling challenges or changes in interests. She'll understand that her dad values the time with her even more than the activity itself, and her confidence in their relationship will increase as a result.

The Father-Daughter Relationship and Work-Life Balance

Work is a necessary part of life; after all, a father's income helps keep his family financially stable and secure. But it's also important to find a work-life balance that ensures fathers can be emotionally available and responsive when their daughters need them. That means being able to manage routines and create a schedule that includes time for work as well as time to intentionally be present with family.

Workplace flexibility and working from home some or all of the time have been huge advantages for many fathers when it comes to work-life balance. Not all employers offer flexible work arrangements, though, and not all jobs can be performed from home. But regardless of whether a dad works from his home some, all, or none of the time, there are ways to try to balance his time and make sure the time he's at home is meaningful.

First, dads can try to organize their day so that the most challenging or emotionally draining tasks are done right away. That way, they'll have the rest of the day to decompress a bit before heading home, and they won't be rushing home to see their daughter right after doing something incredibly difficult that's left them exhausted and grouchy.

Second, it's important for fathers to determine clear expectations about their working hours, their availability, and how much (if any) overtime is acceptable to them. When these boundaries aren't set, it's all too easy for dads to be "on call" and responding to work-related emails and messages at all hours. For a dad to truly prioritize time with his daughter, he needs to define offline time and set an expectation that there are parts of the day when he's simply not available to attend to work-related matters instantly. Dads who work from home should, as much as possible, separate their "working" space and their "home" space. Once they finish with work and shut their office door or turn off their laptop, they've officially checked out of work and checked into time with their daughter.

Finally, remember that being mentally present for a daughter is just as important as being physically present with her. This goes along with the idea of setting boundaries on working hours, but takes it a bit further by reminding fathers that they should leave work behind once they've finished for the day. Even if a dad isn't actually answering his email or sitting at his laptop working on a project, ignoring his daughter or failing to listen to what she's saying because he is thinking about the meetings he has the following day or how to tackle a particularly thorny problem at work is almost as bad. For many dads, it helps to have a simple ritual that signals they're done with work for the day and fully transitioning to family life. That could mean coming home and changing clothes, listening to a favorite song in the car on the way home, or going for a walk around the block after arriving home to decompress and leave work behind.

For dads who struggle to check out of work, setting aside specific tech-free times at home or actually scheduling family time as blocks on the calendar might help. Blocking off father-daughter time on the calendar helps keeps dads accountable and encourages them not to overbook their time, while going tech-free removes the temptation for dads to hop online to "just do one thing real quick" or check emails using their phone.

To wrap up our discussion on the importance of dads who are consistently present to their daughters, I'd like to share the story of a friend whom I'll call Julia. Julia's father had co-founded a business with his brother that eventually grew to become very successful. As the CEO of a multimillion-dollar business, Julia's dad had a lot of work-related responsibilities and traveled fairly regularly. Nevertheless, there was no doubt in Julia's mind that she came first.

Her father made it to almost every single one of her baton competitions, band contests, and piano recitals. The two of them had a weekly routine: pie at the local diner on Friday nights. Her dad was a pilot, and he annually flew her to Chicago for a day each November to walk down the Magnificent Mile and look at the Christmas decorations.

Julia's dad also scheduled family vacations one to two times a year, and he completely unplugged from work for the five to six days that they were on vacation so that his whole focus could be on Julia and her mom.

Julia's dad might have been busy, and his time was in high demand due to his professional obligations, but he was still consistently, persistently present in her life. They had a few routines they shared, and he was great at finding a work-life balance. As a result, Julia has wonderful self-esteem as an adult. She's successful in both her career and her romantic relationship. Her dad laid a foundation for her future simply by being very intentional about being present in her life.

But even dads who have committed to being a stable presence in their daughter's life will see their bond change as their daughter grows older. The father-daughter relationship can and should grow, evolve, and adapt throughout the daughter's life, and we'll look at this more deeply in our next chapter.

Chapter 8:

Growing Together—The Evolution of the Father-Daughter Relationship

Each day of our lives we make deposits in the memory banks of our children.
–Charles R. Swindoll

Like all relationships, the father-daughter bond has to grow and change as time passes. Otherwise, it will remain stagnant and eventually start to fracture; one or both parties might even begin to feel like they've in some way outgrown the other. A daughter's need for trust, security, love, and acceptance will always remain constant. However, the specific ways that she needs her father to be there for her and the type of support that she needs her father to provide will change as she matures.

Together, we'll look at the various stages of life and how a daughter's needs vary throughout her lifetime, as well as ways that fathers can expect their bond to change as their daughter grows. Finally, we'll conclude by talking about some of the ways that the father-daughter relationship can remain strong into adulthood—because no matter how old a girl gets, she's never too old to need her dad.

Adapting to Different Stages of Life

Dads who understand a little bit about child development and the different stages that their daughter will pass through are better equipped to support her as their relationship evolves. In each stage, she has different critical needs, and her dad plays a major role in meeting those needs so that she can continue to thrive.

Early Childhood

Early childhood is often referred to as the formative years, and with good reason. The initial interactions that children experience during this time set the tone for their future relationships, both within and outside their family. During the early years, a dad's role is to build a bond with his daughter and establish trust. It's important for him to be nurturing, playful, and available.

In particular, emotional development has a critical window during the first four years of life (McKitrick, 2020). During this time, a daughter learns to trust, and she learns communication, particularly by reading expressions and listening to voices. This is a major reason why it's so important for her dad to be a constant presence in her life during her early years. One study found a significant correlation between daughters' social-emotional abilities and their fathers' involvement in their life, meaning that more involved fathers led to daughters with higher social-emotional abilities (Harris, 2016).

Other research has shown that a daughter will be more ready for school if she is exposed to more words during her early childhood, so her father can support her development by talking to her and reading to her (Nierengarten, 2019). This time together also helps reinforce their bond and establish a loving, supportive relationship from the start.

Adolescence

As girls move into adolescence, they're also moving away from the total dependence on their parents that they experienced as a very young child and starting to become more and more independent. Many physical, emotional, and social changes take place as a daughter begins her transition out of adulthood. It's a time of critical development in areas like decision-making, establishing moral standards and values, forming supportive relationships, and applying abstract thinking skills.

A father's presence allows him to act as a role model and mentor for her as she is developing these skills. During his daughter's adolescent years, he has to balance authority and guidance with giving his daughter independence and autonomy. He's there to shepherd her through situations she may not be prepared to handle, but he also needs to allow her to start making choices and seeing the impact of her decisions so that she is ready for adulthood.

Adolescence is also a time when anxiety, depression, or other mental health disorders might surface. We've talked at length about how fathers' involvement lessens daughters' risk of mental health challenges, so staying involved in a daughter's life even if she appears to be pulling away is crucial for dads. Knowing that her dad is there for her and available to talk about things can be very comforting for a daughter, even if she sometimes struggles to open up about things.

Another way dads can support their daughters during this time is by admitting that it's new for them, too. Many dads are uncomfortable with the physical and psychological changes that their daughters undergo during puberty. But instead of withdrawing due to this discomfort, being honest with their daughter and letting her know that he's navigating something new, too, is one of the best things that a dad can do. Research suggests that when fathers are actively involved in their daughters' lives, the daughter is less likely to engage in risky or criminal behavior during adolescence (Vanchugova et al., 2022).

While dads generally take the initiative on father-daughter activities during early childhood, it's a good idea for a dad to give his daughter much more input during her adolescent years. While a dad can—and should—still encourage his daughter to spend quality time together, he can let her pick their activities or dictate how they spend their time. This not only increases the chance that she'll be excited about spending time with her dad, but also subtly tells the daughter that her interests and her choices matter. Maintaining a strong bond during the adolescent years can be challenging, but it also presents an opportunity for the father-daughter bond to deepen and mature.

Young Adulthood

As a daughter moves into adulthood, her dad's role shifts from protector to mentor. He is still there in a supportive role, but he needs to adjust his expectations for how deeply he's involved in his daughter's life. She is now responsible for making her own decisions, and he is there in an advisory capacity rather than a decision-making capacity like he was earlier in her life.

Daughters generally face many major life transitions during young adulthood, and dads can be there to provide advice and encouragement. While they aren't in a position to say "This is what you have to do" anymore, they can certainly share their own experiences with their daughter and suggest "If I was in your shoes, this is probably what I would do." Then, he can be his daughter's biggest cheerleader, whether she takes his advice or not.

How Father-Daughter Bonds Change as Daughters Grow Older

It likely won't surprise anyone to hear that daughters perceive their fathers differently during different stages of life. The relationship between fathers and their adult daughters is unique and constantly changing. A daughter's emotional needs evolve as she gets older, and understanding these changes is vital in helping a father maintain a strong bond. Consequently, communication strategies need to evolve as a daughter grows and her needs change.

Communication is something that may not always come naturally to dads. That's compounded by the fact that men and women typically have different communication styles. Men are generally hard-wired to take things at face value, while women are generally hard-wired to reach between the lines and look for the subtext underneath words in addition to what's actually been spoken.

That can make it difficult, at times, for a father to know how to connect with his adult daughter. The rough-and-tumble play that came naturally to him when she was a young child isn't a way that he can relate to a grown daughter, and he may struggle to articulate what he's thinking or feeling. While physical affection can still be expressed in appropriate ways, like hugging good-bye, communication has to become more verbal. Fathers also interact with their grown daughters from a more equal footing than they did when she was a child and he was in charge of her world, offering another nuance in how their communication evolves.

Learning to listen actively, which we discussed in Chapter 1, is an important skill to keep practicing when communicating with an adult daughter. Making an effort to genuinely listen and ask questions indicates to a daughter that her father is interested in her life. For dads who may be overwhelmed by the flow of a conversation or unsure how to keep the conversation going, a good tip is to identify the key word or idea of the last sentence that the daughter said and use that as a basis for a follow-up question.

Often, a father connects with his adult daughter best through shared activities rather than sitting on the couch and having a conversation. Whether that's going golfing, going out to dinner, or going for a hike, having something to do together can often break the ice and allow them to connect on an emotional level. Planning regular outings or activities based on shared interests signals to a daughter that she's just as important in her father's life as she was during her childhood, and his love for her hasn't changed now that she is an adult.

Using "props" can often be another way to start a conversation and build an emotional connection when a daughter has become an adult. Old photos are especially effective. A dad can pull out a stack of family photographs to show his daughter and share some of the background behind the photo with her: what was going on in the photo, how he felt at that time, and why the memory captured by the photo was special to him. Whether it's photos of his own childhood, photos of her childhood, or anything in between, sharing those memories will give the daughter a new look into her father's perspective. Family mementos and heirlooms are also great for this purpose, as they can kick off a conversation about the father's early life and his own family.

Celebrating milestones or achievements, no matter how big or small, is another way for dads and their adult daughters to stay connected. Even just sending a text to recognize that the day is important shows the daughter that her dad is proud of her and thinking about her.

Fathers can find tangible ways to show affection when celebrating a big achievement, or even "just because," as another way to build their relationship with their adult daughter. For instance, sending her a note or a postcard just to let her know that her dad is thinking of her, or sending flowers to mark an important achievement or when he knows that she's been struggling, can mean a lot.

Finally, fathers need to remember that they have to respect their daughter's emerging independence. Fathers naturally want to take on the role of an authority figure, but it's important for them to remember that adult daughters need to make their own decisions and their dad is there to guide them, not to control them. It's okay for a father to share his own experience and make suggestions based on what he's learned during his lifetime, but it's not okay for a father to dictate his adult daughter's course of action or pressure her into making a specific decision.

Daughters may sometimes make choices about their life that are very different from what their father envisioned, and it's important for him to continue to support her. When a dad trusts his daughter's decisions, even if he disagrees with them, he demonstrates that he respects her as an adult. She has to be free to forge her own path and make her own mistakes. Naturally, her father can be there to offer advice and encouragement, but ultimately the decision has to be her own, even if her dad isn't in favor.

As daughters grow and the relationship evolves, fathers should remember that open communication, understanding, and unconditional love are key to maintaining a stable bond. When dads recognize their daughters' emotional needs but also respect their independence, it creates a lasting, meaningful connection that will continue to evolve with time.

Maintaining a Strong Relationship Into Adulthood

Once a daughter has moved into adulthood, she still needs her dad—even if she doesn't verbally express it. From his advice to his steadfast support, it's important for a dad to remain actively involved in his adult daughter's life, within healthy boundaries. A phone call on her birthday and a quick visit at Christmas simply aren't enough, particularly as she first transitions into adulthood. After all, a girl's father has been the most important man in her life for 18 years, and that doesn't stop simply because she legally becomes an adult.

To maintain a strong relationship within appropriate boundaries, open communication is key. When dads criticize, lecture, or judge their daughter, she's likely to close down the lines of communication as a way of protecting herself. No one likes to be criticized, and it's especially painful coming from one of the most important people in her life. A daughter may then be hesitant to broach potentially sensitive topics in the future, further shutting down communication and giving her dad only a surface-level glimpse into what's really going on in her life.

To avoid this situation, dads can practice asking open ended-questions and actively listening to their daughters' answers instead of rushing to a snap judgment. Even if they disagree with her opinions, they should seek to respond from a place of empathy and try to understand why she feels the way that she does before reacting. Not only does this keep the conversation open, but it also conveys to the daughter that her dad respects her as an adult and isn't seeking to establish control over her, as if she were still a child.

I've put together a list of open-ended, conversation-starting questions to help give dads a starting point for opening up the lines of communication with their daughter:

- Tell me a little more about ____ situation. What are your feelings about that?

- What is it like to ____? I've never experienced that, and I'd love to hear your perspective.

- I was thinking back on old memories the other day. What do you remember about ____?

- Tell me, what does a typical day look like for you? What parts of your day do you most enjoy?

- I'm running into ____ (specific issue). How would you handle things if you were in my place?

Remember, too, that if a daughter seems reluctant or hesitant to open up about a specific situation or problem, her dad should respect that boundary. She may not be ready to talk about it yet, or she may need some more time to trust that her dad will actively listen to her without judgment. If dads run into this scenario, sometimes sharing a little bit more about situations they've experienced in their past—struggles they've overcome or sadness they've faced—can help their daughter feel more comfortable sharing a vulnerable part of her life.

Above all, fathers should take on the role of mentor and advisor as their daughter moves into adulthood. That means giving suggestions if asked, allowing them space to spread their wings, and helping them navigate the aftermath of the mistakes they'll inevitably make along the way.

For dads who have a hard time letting go, or who want to continue thinking of themselves as a fatherly protector, it's important to trust that they've given their daughter the most important life lessons and that she has the skills and grit to figure out everything else. Fathers should give advice sparingly and mainly when asked, because giving an adult daughter advice about everything under the sun can be information overload and often causes her to tune out her father's advice entirely.

Instead, dads can save their advice for the things that matter most and let their daughter figure out the smaller stuff on her own. Making a terribly unwise car purchase might have a catastrophic effect on her finances and credit—thus probably meriting some fatherly input—while splurging on new jeans or brunch with friends one too many times in a month will teach a painful but temporary lesson that she can figure out on her own.

In many cases, an adult daughter will relocate far enough away that she's no longer in close geographic proximity to her dad. At other times, she may be in a particularly busy season of life due to her work or her own children. If that's the case, dads can still stay in touch regularly through video calls, texts, and sharing pictures and videos. Even sending a funny picture or a quick text to say hello keeps communication flowing in their relationship and makes it easier to pick right back up where they left off when they have a chance to reconnect in person. Some dads and daughters may find connection in playing games together online or finding a small daily activity they can both do, like completing the day's Wordle and sending each other a photo of their efforts.

There are many ways to stay connected, even when a daughter is no longer living under her dad's roof, and a strong relationship once she becomes an adult should still be a high priority. Adult daughters don't need their dads any less; they just need them in different ways, and continuing to build their relationship as the years pass is mutually beneficial for everyone.

Chapter 9:

The Legacy of a Good Dad

> *It doesn't matter who my father was; it matters who I remember he was.*
> –Anne Sexton

When a father invests in his daughter's life, his legacy lasts far beyond her childhood and even her adulthood. He can have a generational impact and leave a lasting imprint on successive generations of the family. A dad who builds a strong father-daughter relationship helps his daughter become a better parent, assuming she eventually has children. Her children will benefit from their grandfather's relationship with their mom, and there will continue to be a trickle-down effect that positively influences future generations of the family.

The Long-Term Impact of a Father's Love

The emotional and psychological support from a father plays a huge role in shaping his daughter's future, including her future relationships. Dads who are present, encouraging, and understanding help equip their daughters with the tools they need to build supportive connections, strong friendships, and healthy relationships.

At a foundational level, a father's love teaches his daughter what healthy emotional support looks like. When a dad listens, offers guidance, shows affection, and demonstrations genuine interest in her life, he models the type of behavior that a daughter can later draw on to form her own healthy relationships. She'll have learned, from her dad, how to communicate effectively and be emotionally available—thus giving her the foundation she needs to bond strongly with friends, romantic partners, and even her future children.

Daughters of trustworthy, present, available fathers are more confident about expressing their feelings and seeking help when they need it. They know their dad always has their back, and this has allowed them to develop the independence and resilience necessary to provide support for others in their lives. Thus, a cycle of care and connection is created.

As we've seen in previous chapters, daughters generally look to their fathers as examples when forming their own relationships—for better or for worse. It's important to remember that, as the adage goes, values and beliefs are "caught, not taught." Daughters learn from what they see and hear, not what they're told; if their dad tells her that it's important to respect others and communicate kindly but fails to do either of those things in his own relationships, she'll come to believe that respect and kindness aren't nearly as important as her dad says they are, for instance.

When their dad has a strong, respectful bond with their mom, other family members, and friends, the daughter is likely to seek similar dynamics in their future partnerships. They set a standard for how they expect to be treated and how they'll treat others in return. On the other hand, if a daughter sees that her dad's relationships are characterized by conflict and lack of communication, she may internalize that as "normal" and end up replicating those same patterns in her relationships. She perpetuates the cycle for good, if her dad set a strong example, or for bad, if her dad never taught her what a healthy relationship looks like.

A Father's Influence on Generational Cycles

Speaking of perpetuating cycles, a father can have a huge influence on what his family's generational cycles look like. To put it in simple terms, a generational cycle encompasses the habits, attitudes, behaviors, and other traits that get passed down in a family—both positive and negative. Many of us might know families that put a strong emphasis on a particular sport or on philanthropic projects, for instance. These are values that have been passed down from one generation to the next over and over. We may also know families where every generation seems to struggle with substance abuse or failed relationships, and these are also examples of cycles that have been perpetuated from generation to generation.

Interestingly, a 2019 study by Brown and colleagues found that daughters were especially affected by their families' generational cycles of father involvement. In families where fathers had historically had strong relationships with their own fathers, the dads were much more likely to be actively involved in their daughters' lives. This suggests that daughters are particularly likely to be influenced by familial cycles, and so it's important for dads to pay attention to any baggage they may be carrying and to work toward passing along a positive generational cycle to their daughters.

People who recognize an unhealthy generational cycle and actively work to stop it are called "cycle breakers." For example, a dad who recognizes that his father and grandfather struggled to show respect for the women in their lives and consequently works hard to make sure he's deliberate about respecting the women in *his* life is a cycle breaker who's working to create a better future for his family.

This is good news, because it means that all fathers have the chance to create a positive generational cycle even if they're carrying the baggage of negative cycles from previous generations. It takes intentionality and commitment, but it is possible for a father to change a cycle and break any hurtful legacies that are detrimental to his daughter's future. Often, finding a supportive mentor, coach, or therapist provides an invaluable resource for dads who recognize that they've been impacted by harmful generational cycles and want to make a change for their daughters' sake.

For dads who want to break a negative generational cycle, it starts with an honest look at their own upbringing and what habits, attitudes, or behaviors—good and bad—they've internalized as normal. This means figuring out patterns of behavior and communication, identifying what they want to change, and then mapping out small steps toward making those changes.

Good Dads Influence Their Daughters' Parenting

Dads serve as role models for their daughters in many ways, and that's especially true when it comes to teaching their daughters how to approach relationships and parenting. Fathers' interactions with their children, their partner, and their friends and family members give their daughter a blueprint for her own adult life. Daughters pick up parenting skills simply by observing how their father parents. For instance, if he's patient, communicates honestly with his children, and practices empathy, his daughter will learn that these traits are important in parenting.

Going back to the "caught, not taught" adage, daughters learn most of their parenting skills from their own childhood. Their default ways of relating to their children come from how their father and mother related to them. A father who treats his daughter like she matters, shows her that he enjoys spending time with her, and supports her passions and interests will lay the foundation for her to interact with her own children in the same way. Dads who are active parts of their daughters' lives and treat them with empathy and respect—in short, good dads—create daughters who are good moms and treat their own children in the same way.

In addition to watching how their father parents, daughters will also develop their view of relationships and parenting by watching the dynamic between their dad and their mom. If a daughter sees their father treat their mother with respect and kindness, obviously considering her as an equal partner, it teaches the daughter that teamwork and collaboration are a critical part of parenting. She sees that healthy relationships and effective parenting skills are built on mutual support.

On the other hand, a daughter who witnesses negativity or conflict between her parents might struggle to navigate collaborative parenting in the future. She may come to believe that little to no teamwork and poor conflict resolution are normal when it comes to interacting with her partner and parenting her own children. As a result, she is more likely to continue these negative patterns and struggle to parent effectively in the same ways that her own father struggled.

A huge part of parenting is emotional stability; parents who allow their feelings to dictate their response to their children have a hard time parenting effectively. Good dads help create emotional stability, and in turn they set their daughter up to create her own stable, emotionally healthy family in the future. Fathers who are consistently present, both physically and mentally, create a stable environment in the home.

Fathers who treat their families with respect and kindness take this even further by creating a sense of emotional security. Their daughters don't have to worry about being belittled or criticized by their dad, so they feel safe. This sense of safety, in turn, will be pulled forward into the daughter's own family. She's seen what emotionally stability looks like firsthand and lived it out during her childhood, so she is equipped to provide a similar environment for her own children.

One long-term study found that spending one-on-one time with their father was a direct predictor of whether children would grow up to demonstrate a strong sense of empathy and compassion (Koerstner et al., 1990). Adults who exhibited these traits were highly likely to have had fathers who were involved in their lives. Dads who carve out time to spend with their daughters will raise girls who become empathetic, caring parents in their own regard.

Another study, although done on mice, revealed that good parenting can actually cause chemical changes in brain DNA that last for multiple generations. In this study, mice cared for by attentive parent mice who licked them often and thoroughly were later better parents themselves and so were their children, the second generation. Preliminary studies on human brains show similar chemical patterns between abused children and neglected mice, intimating that our human brains may also actually change at a chemical level due to good (or bad) parenting, and that these changes can be passed to the next generation (Winston & Chicot, 2016). In short, how dads parent their daughters matters not just for the daughter, but also for her children.

The Lasting Imprint of a Father's Guidance

A father's guidance, love, and support doesn't end when his daughter becomes a mature adult herself, or even when he passes away. The advice, life lessons, and wisdom that he imparted during her childhood, teenage years, and early adulthood will continue to influence her throughout her life.

I'd like to illustrate just how overarching a father's impact can be by sharing a couple stories of women who have found their father's advice guiding them in their later years, including after he's passed away. The values and principles he instilled in each of them have served as a foundational core throughout their adult years, even if not always consciously.

Tricia's father was an extremely orderly, organized man who believed firmly that everything had a place and everything should stay in its place. She rebelled against this penchant for order a bit during her teenage years, but as she matured, she found herself returning to her father's organized, logical principles. From small, fairly insignificant things like organizing her closet by color to more important concerns like keeping detailed financial records organized in a filing cabinet, Tricia's affairs became almost as methodical as her dad's.

She gained a reputation for her efficiency and attention to detail at work, and this resulted in several promotions throughout the years because she'd earned a lot of trust from her employer due to the thoroughness of her work. Although Tricia's father passed away many years ago, she still cleans her garden tools before storing them away each fall and files the service records for her vehicle in color-coded folders just like her dad taught her. The systems, principles, and orderly habits that her dad instilled in her during childhood still guide her daily habits today.

Lisa's dad was an excellent businessman with disciplined financial habits. Although he'd started his own small business, he drove unassuming vehicles, took modest vacations, and lived quite simply. The "latest and greatest" never appealed to him; he frequently told

Lisa, "Why do I need to buy that? The one I have is perfectly fine." In fact, it wasn't until after his death that Lisa truly grasped just how financially successful her father had been. He'd been quietly giving substantial sums of money to charitable causes, and he had a very comfortable financial cushion in place so that Lisa's mom would have the resources she needed for any future medical care or other expenses.

Lisa began to realize just how much her father had instilled those same values in her when she did her tax return the year her father died. She looked at her finances in a new light and realized that she, too, had dedicated a significant portion of her income to philanthropic efforts that were important to her. She lived well within her means and had a robust savings account. Her dad had deeply ingrained one of his core principles into her: money was a tool, and it was important to use it wisely.

In addition, Lisa realized how much stability and security she'd felt as a child because her father had his finances in order and was never stressed about money. They may not have lived luxuriously, but her parents didn't fight about finances or get anxious about paying for "extras." They simply took care of their bills without worrying, and then spent time with Lisa and her siblings. This was a huge gift, and this stability was something Lisa had unwittingly passed on to her own family. She and her husband didn't live luxuriously, either, but they had a very comfortable life and their finances were never a source of stress or division within their home.

Daughters of good dads often become positive role models not just within their families, but also within their communities. A good dad does a lot to equip his daughter for a leadership role. Fathers nurture independence, instill confidence, and encourage perseverance. They're also typically good at delegation—most dads naturally divide up household chores and expect each person in the family or group to do their part. Above all, a good dad who holds firm to his convictions inspires his daughter to do the same. Taken together, all of these qualities empower daughters to lead.

My dear friend Karen is one such leader. When she was a child, her dad encouraged her to figure things out and allowed her to make a lot of mistakes. Then, he'd appear to help her work through the problem and reward her perseverance with a sweet treat. He also encouraged her to ask others for help, especially in areas where they were good at something and she struggled. As a result, Karen developed a lot of character traits that have served her well in her work as the board president of a community organization and chairwoman of a highly anticipated annual event. She delegates easily, can assess problems calmly and accurately, makes decisions quickly, and has the confidence to defend her choices without becoming defensive or hostile. Above all, Karen has a vision of what she wants the organization and event to look like, and she holds firmly to those convictions as her guiding principle for the decisions she makes and the planning she does.

Dads have an incredibly important role to play in their daughters' lives, with an impact that stretches across generations. His relationship with his daughter arguably leaves a much greater legacy than any financial or professional success he has during his lifetime. But if that makes dads feel like there's much too much pressure on them to build up their father-daughter relationship, I'm here to offer some practical advice for being the best dad possible in our next chapter.

Chapter 10:

Lessons for Fathers—How to Be the Best Dad You Can Be

Fathering is not something perfect men do, but something that perfects the man.
—Frank Pittman

As we finish exploring the many ways that fathers can impact their daughters' lives by being present, supportive, and loving, we'll end with some practical tips to help dads continue learning and growing. By avoiding common pitfalls and learning from others' mistakes, fathers can keep improving and become the best dad that they can possibly be.

Advice for Current and Future Fathers

The best advice often comes from other fathers who have made meaningful changes and seen their relationship with their daughter improve as a result. The following nuggets of wisdom were collected from dads, specifically for other dads:

- **Love is an action, not a feeling:** Think about love as a verb, and work on actively creating it in the home. Love isn't magically sustained by itself; it has to be promoted through words and actions.

- **When you're present, be present:** Even if schedule conflicts prevent a dad from attending every single one of his daughter's activities, he can prioritize being actively there when he's able to be present. Being at an event but spending half the time sending emails, making phone calls, or ignoring what's going on is effectively no better than not attending at all. When a father is at an event, staying engaged and making his presence at the event his top priority will speak volumes to his daughter.

- **Each child is unique, and the way you parent each child will be unique, too:** Fathers who have more than one daughter will very likely find that while the basic principles of love, support, encouragement, and so on remain the same, the way they interact with and relate to each daughter will look a little different. They're unique individuals with different personalities and communication styles, so their dad will have to adapt accordingly and treat them as individuals rather than carbon copies of each other.

- **Be specific and intentional with your words:** This is particularly applicable when a daughter is young. Using specific language to indicate feelings and intentions removes confusion and models for a daughter how to communicate her needs and wants. "Please put your blocks on the shelf" is much more effective than "Pick up this mess," and "It looks like you're overwhelmed and need a moment to calm down" works a lot better than "Stop shrieking."

- **Remember that your daughter is always learning something from you:** Daughters watch their fathers and listen to what they say—and what they don't do and don't say. Dads are teachers when they mean to be as well as when they don't mean to be, and they should be aware that their daughters are always absorbing both the intentional and unintentional lessons.

- **It's okay to struggle. Forgive yourself, and apologize when needed:** We're all human, and all dads will fail from time to time. That doesn't mean they are bad fathers. It just means they are still learning and growing, and they made a mistake along the way. Dads need to remember to forgive themselves so that they don't get stuck in shame and guilt. As part of that process, sometimes it's necessary to apologize to their daughter for missing her big soccer game, or letting emotions get out of control and yelling, or getting distracted by the phone instead of playing with her. Apologies help fathers and daughters move forward, and they teach daughters an important lesson about seeking forgiveness and moving on from mistakes.

One thing we've talked about a lot throughout these chapters is communication. This is an area that doesn't come intuitively to a lot of dads, even though it's incredibly important to the father-daughter relationship. As we've learned, it's incredibly important for dads to model the positive communication that they want their daughters to experience later in life. But how does a dad do that? I'd like to share some concrete ideas of positive, effective communication versus negative, ineffective communication to help show fathers how some small, simple tweaks can radically change the way they relate to their daughters:

- Instead of "How was your day?" ask daughters specific questions that will allow them to share the little details of their day, like:

    - *What was something you learned today?*

    - *What was the most interesting thing that happened at recess?*

    - *Who did you see practice kindness today?*

    - *If you could have a do-over on anything that happened today, what would it be?*

- Instead of "Good work," praise something specific and tangible, like:

    - *Great job switching hands on your dribble. I can see you've been practicing that.*

- *I'm really proud of how neatly you stacked those toys back on the shelf.*

- *I can tell you worked really hard to memorize your spelling words this week because of how quickly you just spelled them all for me.*

• Instead of "Need help?" ask about specific things a daughter appears to be struggling with, but might be too embarrassed to admit:

- *Would you like to look at that science homework together? Some of those questions look a little tricky, and it might help if we talk them through together.*

- *It looks like you're having a hard time getting those pieces to stick together. Can I show you another way you could try doing it?*

- *Would you like to practice fielding some ground balls together? I'd love to show you a trick that my dad taught me for handling tricky hops.*

• Instead of "Stop it!" tell a daughter what specific behavior isn't okay and why:

- *Take your hands off your brother. I know you don't like when people hit you, and other people don't like being hit, either. It hurts them.*

- *Put the toys down. Remember that in our family, we do not throw toys because they could break or hurt someone. We put them down nicely.*

- *Try saying that again. In our family, we speak kindly and respectfully.*

Specific, intentional language is the common denominator in the examples above. Being clear about expectations, highlighting something concrete and tangible, and helping a daughter name what she's feeling and experiencing can take a father's communication from "meh" to "WOW!" in no time at all.

Setting Fair, Respectful Boundaries

While communication is a common sticking point for many dads, setting fair boundaries is another pitfall for dads to be aware of. It's important to create boundaries that are fair and promote respect, but without becoming overly strict and authoritarian. In other words, it's a balancing act! Too many rules can stand in the way of forming a true relationship and lead to rebellion. On the flip side, overindulging a daughter and having no rules at all hinders her growth and learning as well as sets unrealistic expectations about what life is like.

To help avoid these pitfalls, think about the purpose of rules and boundaries. They're meant to keep people safe and secure so that they have the freedom to go about their lives. For instance, a speed limit helps keep people safe on the road so they are free to drive without fear. The rules and expectations that a father sets for his daughter should function in the same way. They're meant to keep her safe while still allowing her the freedom to learn and grow.

Boundaries should be firm, but they should be thoughtful and fair. Fathers should think about what is, to them, non-negotiable. That might include things like bedtime or curfew, kindness, respect for others' property, or commitment to schoolwork. The boundary or expectation should be made clear to their daughter and then kept consistent. She may not like it at first, and so it's important for her dad to remain committed to the boundary and to gently but firmly enforce the limits.

This actually frees up both the father and daughter to enjoy each other's presence and focus on the moment. Having clear, consistent boundaries forestalls a lot of arguments and removes the conflict that often comes with negotiations. For instance, if a dad sets a boundary around bedtime and is consistent in expecting his daughter to go to bed at 8:30 p.m., they can enjoy the evening together without dread of the upcoming "bedtime battle."

As the daughter grows and matures, the boundaries may need to change a little bit. Things like bedtimes and curfews can shift, and the daughter can start taking on more responsibility for fulfilling her commitments. Dads can keep the boundaries in place but respect the daughter's maturity by having open conversations about the expectations that are in place and asking for her feedback about boundaries that may need to be reconsidered now that she is older. He may still be the one who ultimately makes the decision, but taking her opinion into account shows the daughter that she's respected and trusted.

Along with learning to set clear but fair boundaries, fathers also need to think about the balancing act between being too restrictive and too overindulgent. There are shortcomings associated with both being too strict and being too lenient, so it's important to find the middle ground.

Overindulging a daughter, or being too lenient, means giving her everything she wants regardless of whether she truly needs it, allowing her to do things that are not appropriate for her age or level of development, or catering to her every whim in such a way that she never has the chance to learn life lessons. When a daughter is overindulged, she often becomes entitled, irresponsible, or disrespectful and is more likely to struggle with low self-control, a lack of meaningful relationships, depression, and poorly managing money as an adult (Bredehoft, 2022). It can be hard for a father to watch his daughter struggle, but learning to tackle and overcome age-appropriate challenges is a huge part of childhood development, and understanding the difference in needs versus wants is critical for success in adulthood. When a father overindulges his daughter, he unintentionally deprives her of these two crucial learning opportunities.

On the other hand, fathers who are too strict and set extremely stringent rules in order to exert control jeopardize their relationship with their daughter. She may end up rejecting her dad and everything he values as an act of rebellion against an overly restrictive upbringing, and that can also lead to problems in adulthood. Structure is important, but being overly rigid and failing to account for the relationship first creates problems between the father and daughter that may follow her into her adult years.

Continual Improvement as a Father

Setting boundaries and finding the balance between rules and leniency is a delicate process, and it's an area where many fathers find themselves constantly adjusting and improving. This is also an important part of the father-daughter relationship as a whole. No father is perfect, so it stands to reason that every father has the opportunity to assess himself regularly and seek out areas where he can improve his parenting and his relationship with his daughter.

Taking a clear, honest look at what's going well and what's not working is really important for dads. Without doing this, it's hard to make changes and improve father-daughter interactions. Dads who are committed to making improvements should start by assessing themselves on a regular basis and using those assessments to set goals for the immediate future.

One of the best ways for a dad to self-assess is to seek out feedback. His daughter is a fantastic source, but his partner, family, and friends may also have insights to share that he can use to improve his relationship with his daughter. Dads can think about asking for feedback in specific areas like communication, the quality of the time they spend together, the frequency of their interaction, or any other category that makes sense for them.

Once the feedback has been received, it's critical to put it into use. Feedback without action is just information; feedback with action turns into improvement. Dads can use the feedback they get to set goals following the SMART framework: Specific, Measurable, Achievable, Relevant, and Time-Sensitive.

For example, let's say a dad gets some feedback from his daughter that she doesn't feel like there's much value in the time they spend together because he is usually on his phone. Her dad could use this feedback to set a SMART goal that looks something like the following:

- **Specific:** He can commit to putting his phone in another room or turning it off when he's hanging out with his daughter.

- **Measurable:** He could notate on the calendar each time he spends time with his daughter without the phone to track how he's doing.

- **Achievable:** He can easily spend an hour or two offline a few times a week, so this goal doesn't have anything that would stand in the way of accomplishing it.

- **Relevant:** His daughter's main concern with the quality of time they spend together is that her dad is distracted by his phone, so removing the phone from the picture entirely is a direct response to her feedback.

- **Time-Sensitive:** He could resolve to be very intentional about this goal for the next month and then check back in with his daughter to see if she's noticed a difference.

For dads who aren't sure where to begin, Dr. Michelle Watson Canfield has a self-assessment test called "The Dialed-In Dad Checklist" on her website, www.drmichellewatson.com. This resource might help jump-start some ideas and get the ball rolling in terms of thinking about how to improve as a dad and strengthen the father-daughter relationship.

Further Resources

Fatherhood isn't meant to be a solo journey, and it's important to be a lifelong learner. Dads and their daughters will both benefit when fathers commit to educating themselves, seeking out information, and continually improving. Books, blogs, and other online resources can be great sources of information, particularly the sites run by these groups:

- **National Fatherhood Initiative:** www.fatherhood.org

- **National Responsible Fatherhood Clearinghouse:** www.fatherhood.gov

- **National Center for Fathering:** www.fathers.com

One of the most impactful things a dad can do is to build a support network of other fathers who can share advice and experiences. Seeking out a mentor—a more experienced father with a lot of wisdom and information to offer—is also important, especially if the dad didn't have a strong father figure in their own life growing up. After all, dads need someone who can help teach them how to be a dad; if they didn't get this from their own father, it's wise to seek help from someone else.

Above all, dads should stay willing to be flexible and adaptable as they learn and as their daughter grows and matures. Like so many other things in life, the only constant thing about fatherhood is that it's going to change. The best dads are prepared, willing, and able to change and grow so that their daughters have room to soar.

Conclusion

She did not stand alone, but what stood behind her, the most potent moral force in her life, was the love of her father.
–Harper Lee

Being a father is an incredible journey, and dads have a profound impact on their daughters' lives. We've seen how a dad can influence just about every aspect of his daughter's life, from her earliest days into her adult years. Dads have a key role to play in providing emotional support, helping develop independence and resilience, and giving their daughters the tools to succeed in life. In short, dads are irreplaceable!

Throughout these chapters, we've taken a deep dive into why dads matter, how they impact their daughters, and what they can do to create an unbreakable father-daughter bond. Now, it's time for dads to take the next step, put these principles into practice, and make a lasting difference in their daughters' lives.

That starts today, regardless of whether a dad is parenting a toddler, teenager, or any age in between. It's even applicable for fathers of adult daughters. A few small, simple, daily steps can lead to significant change. By using the knowledge gained from these pages to make an effort in a few key areas, dads can begin to transform their relationship with their daughters.

First, dads should remember the power of listening actively. They can make a habit of putting away distractions and genuinely hearing their daughter to show her that her thoughts and feelings are valued. Next, it's important for dads to carve out quality time for their daughters on a regular basis. It doesn't matter what they do together; the important thing is that they spend dedicated one-on-one time with each other.

Then, dads shouldn't underestimate the power of their love and affection. Saying "I love you" daily, giving daughters a hug or a high-five, or otherwise tangibly expressing love go a long way toward reinforcing a daughter's sense of self-worth and security. Additionally, fathers are always teaching. Use small, daily moments to share life lessons, pass along values, and teach essential skills. The lessons that a daughter learns from her dad will be with her for life, so it's important for dads to stay intentional about what they are teaching.

Finally, dads are role models. Daughters notice what their dads do even more than they hear what their dad says. Fathers who treat their daughters, their families, their friends, and everyone they meet with respect and kindness provide their daughters with an incredible foundation for the future.

Remember that every day is a chance for a dad to reinforce and strengthen his connection with his daughter. Simple repeated actions often have a much stronger impact than grand but infrequent gestures; there's an incredible power that comes from a dad who simply shows up for his daughter every single day no matter what else is going on in his life. There's no single way to be the perfect dad, but the best dads all have a few things in common. Being present to their daughters, encouraging them, and pouring into them are the uniting factors.

I'd like to challenge all fathers reading this to make a promise to themselves and their daughters: Take simple, intentional actions each day that will commit to growing the relationship. A small investment of time today will pay off hugely down the road, when the daughter's personal and professional life are tremendously impacted as a result.

I hope this book has given you some key takeaways and new insights that will help you better understand and navigate your own father-daughter interactions. Your experience is unique and valuable, and I encourage you to leave a review to share how the ideas in these pages have motivated, inspired, or challenged you to keep growing.

Ultimately, the key thing to keep in mind is the legacy that dads want to leave their daughters. The life lessons and values that a dad instills in his daughter through their daily interactions will influence how she understands relationships, her sense of self-worth, and her emotional well-being throughout the rest of her life.

That doesn't mean a dad has to be perfect, by any means. He just has to be willing to keep learning, keep growing, and keep showing up. When a father is committed to connecting with his daughter and encouraging her dreams, he has a profoundly positive impact despite the mistakes he'll inevitably make along the way. In the end, the sum will definitely be greater than the parts.

Dads have the power to make a difference in their daughters' lives, and that difference can start today. It's never too late to provide love, encouragement, and guidance. Seize daily opportunities to connect, and embrace the chance to build a meaningful father-daughter relationship that will last for a lifetime.

References

Atkins, S. (2023, June 26). *The importance of father-child bonding.* Sue Atkins The Parenting Expert. https://sueatkinsparentingcoach.com/2023/06/the-importance-of-father-child-bonding/

Bernstein, J. (2024, March 10). *How to help your adult child open up and connect.* Psychology Today. https://www.psychologytoday.com/us/blog/liking-the-child-you-love/202403/how-to-help-your-adult-child-open-up-and-connect

Blouin, M. (2022, April 15). *Research review shows self-esteem has long-term benefits.* UC Davis. https://www.ucdavis.edu/curiosity/news/research-review-shows-self-esteem-has-long-term-benefits

Boggs, W. (n.d.). In Lemire, S. (2024, June 12), *78 father-daughter quotes that speak to their unbreakable bond.* Today. https://www.today.com/life/holidays/father-daughter-quotes-rcna27545

Bohn, K. (2021, August 2). *Closeness with dads may play a special role in how kids weather adolescence.* Penn State. https://www.psu.edu/news/research/story/closeness-dads-may-play-special-role-how-kids-weather-adolescence

Bredehoft, D. J. (2022, April 22). *16 ways overindulging your child can harm them in the future.* Psychology Today. https://www.psychologytoday.com/us/blog/the-age-of-overindulgence/202204/16-ways-overindulging-your-child-can-harm-them-in-the-future

Brown, C. A. (2015, January 13). *5 easy ways dads can get involved in their child's education.* National Fatherhood Initiative. https://www.fatherhood.org/championing-fatherhood/5-easy-ways-dads-can-get-involved-in-their-childs-education

Brown, G. L., Kogan, S. M., & Kim, J. (2017, February). From fathers to sons: the intergenerational transmission of parenting behavior among African American young men. *Family Process, 57*(1), 165–180. https://doi.org/10.1111/famp.12273

Brown, P. (n.d.). In Lemire, S. (2024, June 12), *78 father-daughter quotes that speak to their unbreakable bond.* Today. https://www.today.com/life/holidays/father-daughter-quotes-rcna27545

Christensen, M. (2022, September 26). *44 pieces of parenting advice from dads who've been there.* Fatherly. https://www.fatherly.com/life/life-changing-parenting-advice-dads

Clark, T. (2021, December 5). *How do we safeguard our kids from toxic relationships?* The We Spot. https://thewespot.com/how-do-we-safeguard-our-kids-from-toxic-relationships/

Carroll, J. S. (2024, June 12). *We need dads more than ever.* Institute for Family Studies. https://ifstudies.org/blog/we-need-dads-more-than-ever

Culpin, I., Heuvelman, H., Raj, D., Pearson, R. M., Joinson, C., Heron, J., Evans, J., & Kwong, A. S. F. (2022, October 1). Father absence and trajectories of offspring mental health across adolescence and young adulthood: Findings from a UK-birth cohort. *Journal of Affective Disorders, 314.* 150-159. https://doi.org/10.1016%2Fj.jad.2022.07.016

Dads, give your daughters the gift of financial strength. (2019, June 19). Singer Wealth Management. https://singerwealthmanagement.com/dads-give-your-daughters-the-gift-of-financial-strength/

Dads you matter too! Strengthening the father-daughter bond. (n.d.). Alpine Academy. https://alpineacademy.org/dads-you-matter-too-strengthening-the-father-daughter-bond/

Daniel, J. (2019, June 20). *the impact of the absent father on daughters.* Wounds to Scars. https://woundstoscars.com/the-impact-of-the-absent-father-on-daughters/

Dobson, J. (n.d.). In Lemire, S. (2024, June 12), *78 father-daughter quotes that speak to their unbreakable bond.* Today. https://www.today.com/life/holidays/father-daughter-quotes-rcna27545

Dobson, J. (n.d.). *When daughters need daddy most.* Dobson Digital Library. https://dobsonlibrary.com/resource/article/dabb631c-eaab-4f64-a581-ac6dd6abbba8

Dominguez, L. F. (2022, June 14). *101 dad and daughter activities, games, and fun ideas.* Spanish Homeschool Academy. https://www.spanish.academy/blog/101-dad-and-daughter-activities-games-and-fun-ideas/

Dupre, D. A. (2021, September 8). *Young adult children still need their fathers too.* Hope for Widows Foundation. https://hopeforwidows.org/2021/09/young-adult-children-still-need-their-fathers-too/

8 steps to set compassionate & kind boundaries with young children. (n.d.). Heart-Mind Online. https://heartmindonline.org/resources/8-steps-to-set-compassionate-kind-boundaries-with-young-children

Father daughter relationships | Why girls desperately need their dad. (n.d.). Simply Midori. https://simplymidori.com/father-daughter-relationships/

Father's day financial literacy: Talk to your kids about money. (2023, June 15). Abeona Wealth. https://abeonawealth.com/fathers-day-financial-literacy-talk-to-your-kids-about-money/

A father's impact on child development. (2023, May 12). All For Kids. https://www.allforkids.org/news/blog/a-fathers-impact-on-child-development/

Fathers play an important role in child development. (n.d.). KidCentral TN. https://www.kidcentraltn.com/development/0-12-months/fathers-play-an-important-role-in-child-development.html

Flouri, E., & Buchanan, A. (2003, February). The role of father involvement in child's later mental health. *Journal of Adolescence, 26*(1), 63-78. https://doi.org/10.1016/S0140-1971(02)00116-1

Flowers, L. (2019, June 18). *Season of challenges calls for new outlook on change.* Lois Flowers. https://www.loisflowers.com/how-my-dad-influenced-my-life/

Foster, B. L. (2005, October 1). *Fathers and daughters.* Washingtonian. https://www.washingtonian.com/2005/10/01/fathers-and-daughters/

Gallo, A. (2023, September 6). *6 little things you can do every day to make your child more independent.* Parents. https://www.parents.com/kids/development/little-things-you-can-do-every-day-to-make-your-child-more-independent/

Gonzalez, A. (2021, June 19). *Leadership and life lessons I learned from my dad.* Transformative Conversations. https://www.transformativeconversations.com/blog/leadership-from-dad/2021-06-19

Haaz, D. H., Kneavel, M., & Browning, S. W. (2014, February). The father-daughter relationship and intimacy in the marriages of daughters of divorce. *Journal of Divorce and Remarriage, 55*(2), 164-177. http://dx.doi.org/10.1080/10502556.2013.871962

Hall, L. (2023, March 11). First things first: What are generational cycles, and why do they matter? *Chattanooga Times Free Press.* https://www.timesfreepress.com/news/2023/mar/11/what-are-generational-cycles-tfp/

Hall, S. (2009). Paternal influences on daughters' heterosexual relationship socialization: Attachment style and disposition toward marriage. *Family Science Review, 14*(2). https://www.familyscienceassociation.org/wp-content/uploads/2021/07/2009-14-2-Paternal-influences-on-daughters-heterosexual-relationship-socialization_Scott-Hall-Final.pdf

Harris, R. D. (2016, Spring). A meta-analysis on father involvement and early child social-emotional development. *Applied Psychology Opus.* https://wp.nyu.edu/steinhardt-appsych_opus/a-meta-analysis-on-father-involvement-and-early-childhood-social-emotional-development/

Healing from the father wound. (2023, June 20). Haven Mental Health Counseling. https://havenmhc.com/musings/2023/6/20/healing-from-the-father-wound

Health benefits of having a routine. (2022, March). Northwestern Medicine. https://www.nm.org/healthbeat/healthy-tips/health-benefits-of-having-a-routine#:~:text=An%20effective%20routine%20can%20help

Hope for healing the wound of an absent father or divorce. (2016, March 2). Dr. Rachel Glik. https://www.drrachelglik.com/blog-posts/2016/3/2/hope-for-healing-the-wound-of-an-absent-father

How abuse in childhood affects your relationships as an adult. (n.d.). Lionhearted Counseling. https://www.lionheartedcounseling.com/trauma-therapy/how-abuse-in-childhood-affects-your-relationships-as-an-adult

How dads can solve problems for their family. (n.d.). The Daily Dad. https://dads4kids.org.au/how-dads-can-solve-problems-for-their-family/

How parents can instill a growth mindset at home. (n.d.). Mindset Works. https://www.mindsetworks.com/parents/growth-mindset-parenting

How parents can teach kids financial literacy while learning it ourselves. (n.d.). Fitzsimons. https://www.fitzsimonscu.com/how-parents-can-teach-kids-financial-literacy-while-learning-it-ourselves/

How to communicate better with your grown child. (n.d.). Newport Institute. https://www.newportinstitute.com/resources/family-connection/communicate-grown-child/

The impact of fathers on daughters: Nurturing confidence and independence. (2023, December 7). Dear Fathers. https://dearfathers.com/2023/12/the-impact-of-fathers-on-daughters-nurturing-confidence-and-independence/

The importance of father daughter relationships. (2019, June 12). All For Kids. https://www.allforkids.org/news/blog/the-importance-of-father-daughter-relationships/

Islamiah, N., Breinholst, S., Walczak, M. A., & Esbjørn, B. E. (2023, January 4). The role of fathers in children's emotion regulation development: A systematic review. *Infant and Child Development, 32*(2), e2397. https://doi.org/10.1002/icd.2397

Ivy Exec. (2024, October 18). *8 (realistic) ways working dads can achieve work-life balance.* Excelsior University. https://communities.excelsior.edu/blog/2024/10/18/8-realistic-ways-working-dads-can-achieve-work-life-balance/

Jacobson, R. (2024, March 1). *10 tips to help dads and daughters stay close.* Child Mind Institute. https://childmind.org/article/10-tips-help-dads-daughters-stay-close/

Jarecke-Chang, K. (2023, June 12). *37 fun father-daughter activities to build special memories.* TinyBeans. https://tinybeans.com/father-daughter-activities/

Jessee, V., & Adamsons, K. (2018). Father involvement and father-child relationship quality: An intergenerational perspective. *Parenting, Science and Practice, 18*(1), 28–44. https://doi.org/10.1080/15295192.2018.1405700

Jeynes, W. (2018, June 13). *Acknowledging the unique role of fathers.* Institute for Family Studies. https://ifstudies.org/blog/acknowledging-the-unique-role-of-fathers

Johnson III, Amos. (n.d.) Fathers.com. https://fathers.com/blog/nurturance/all-children-need-affirmation/

Jules, A. (2016, May 19). How to raise independent daughters. *TIME*. https://time.com/4318761/fatherhood-masculinity-raising-daughters/

Kiderlin, S. (2023, September 26). Involved dads help kids succeed in school: Here's how. CNBC Make It. https://www.cnbc.com/2023/09/26/dads-have-a-unique-effect-on-kids-attainment-heres-how.html

Koerstner, R., Franz, C., & Weinberger, J. (1990). The family origins of empathic concern: A 26-year longitudinal study. *Journal of Personality and Social Psychology, 58*(4), 709–717. https://psycnet.apa.org/doi/10.1037/0022-3514.58.4.709

Koop, D. (2012, June 17). Fathers and the power of validation. *Upwards Church*. https://upwards.blog/2012/06/17/fathers-and-the-power-of-validation/

Kromberg, J. (2013, July 1). *How dads shape daughters' relationships*. Psychology Today. https://www.psychologytoday.com/intl/blog/inside-out/201307/how-dads-shape-daughters-relationships

Kruk, E. (2012, May 23). *Father absence, father deficit, father hunger*. Psychology Today. https://www.psychologytoday.com/us/blog/co-parenting-after-divorce/201205/father-absence-father-deficit-father-hunger

Lakhani, S. (n.d.). *Helping children cope with major life changes.* Calgary's Child. https://www.calgaryschild.com/parenting/all-ages/2406-beginnings-and-endings-helping-children-cope-with-major-life-changes

Langlois, C. (2014, January 5). *Fathers, daughters & learning self-esteem.* PsychCentral. https://psychcentral.com/blog/fathers-daughters-learning-self-esteem#1

Lasting impressions: A father's model. (n.d.). Fathers.com. https://fathers.com/blog/consistency/lasting-impressions-a-fathers-model/

Lee, H. (n.d.). In Lemire, S. (2024, June 12), *78 father-daughter quotes that speak to their unbreakable bond.* Today. https://www.today.com/life/holidays/father-daughter-quotes-rcna27545

Lee, R. (2015, June 9). *Fathers are the standard bearer for their daughters.* HuffPost. https://www.huffpost.com/entry/fathers-are-the-standard-bearers-for-their-daughters_b_7540190

Luo, G., Wang, L.-G., & Gao, W.-B. (2011, September 9). The influence of the absence of fathers and the timing of separation on anxiety and self-esteem of adolescents: A cross-sectional survey. *Child: Care, Health and Development, 38*(5), 723-731. https://onlinelibrary.wiley.com/doi/abs/10.1111/j.1365-2214.2011.01304.x

Machin, A. (2019, July 16). *Dads and daughters.* Anna Machin. https://annamachin.com/dads-and-daughters/

McKitrick, A. (2020, August 4). *Critical periods of development in the first years of your child's life*. Nurtured Noggins. https://nurturednoggins.com/critical-periods-of-development-in-the-first-years-of-your-childs-life/

McMinn, T. (2024, February 26). *Parenting tips for dads: Creating trust-filled relationships with kids*. Dadhood. https://www.dadhood.co/post/parenting-tips-for-dads-creating-trust-filled-relationships-with-kids

Minnelli, L. (n.d.). In Lemire, S. (2024, June 12), *78 father-daughter quotes that speak to their unbreakable bond*. Today. https://www.today.com/life/holidays/father-daughter-quotes-rcna27545

Mitchard, J. (2022, November 29). *How to be a good parent after a bad childhood*. Parents. https://www.parents.com/parenting/better-parenting/advice/how-to-be-a-good-parent-after-a-bad-childhood/

Morgan, H. R. (2021, January 8). *What the best dads do to raise badass daughters*. Forbes. https://www.forbes.com/sites/heathermorgan/2019/06/14/best-dads-raise-badass-daughters/

Mott, L. (2022, June 3). *Three amazing dads on how to empower your daughter financially*. Her Money. https://hermoney.com/connect/family/three-amazing-dads-on-how-to-empower-your-daughter-financially/

Nelson, C. (2023, May 10). *The 4 types of parenting styles: What style is right for you?* Mayo Clinic Press. https://mcpress.mayoclinic.org/parenting/what-parenting-style-is-right-for-you/

Nguyen, J. (2017, August 23). *How a dad shapes his daughter's future love life.* Sacred Potential. https://www.sacredpotential.com/how-a-dad-shapes-his-daughters-future-love-life/

Nielsen, L. (2014, June 3). *How dads affect their daughters into adulthood.* Institute for Family Studies. https://ifstudies.org/blog/how-dads-affect-their-daughters-into-adulthood

Nielsen, L. (2022). *Relational aspects of parental involvement to support educational outcomes.* Routledge.

Nierengarten, M. B. (2019, June 12). *Fathers' influence on development and well-being of children.* Contemporary Pediatrics. https://www.contemporarypediatrics.com/view/fathers-influence-development-and-well-being-children

Parker-Pope, T. (2009, February 23). More dads influence daughters' career paths. *The New York Times.* https://archive.nytimes.com/well.blogs.nytimes.com/2009/02/23/more-dads-influence-daughters-career-path/

Pittman, F. (n.d.). In Lemire, S. (2024, June 12), *78 father-daughter quotes that speak to their unbreakable bond.* Today. https://www.today.com/life/holidays/father-daughter-quotes-rcna27545

Plett, H. (2023, August 24). Let go, dear parent (Tips for when your child moves away). *Heather Plett*. https://heatherplett.com/2023/08/let-go-dear-parent-when-your-child-moves-away/

Poindexter, L. (n.d.). In Lemire, S. (2024, June 12), *78 father-daughter quotes that speak to their unbreakable bond*. Today. https://www.today.com/life/holidays/father-daughter-quotes-rcna27545

Porter, D. (2023, September 21). *10 benefits of a strong father-daughter relationship*. Marriage.com. https://www.marriage.com/advice/parenting/father-daughter-relationship/

Ratnadeepak, M. (n.d.). In Lemire, S. (2024, June 12), *78 father-daughter quotes that speak to their unbreakable bond*. Today. https://www.today.com/life/holidays/father-daughter-quotes-rcna27545

Roberts, N. (2020, June 21). *Strong father-daughter relationships lead to healthier, happier women*. Forbes. https://www.forbes.com/sites/nicolefisher/2020/06/21/strong-father-daughter-relationships-lead-to-healthier-happier-women/

Sanford, T. L. (n.d.) *Importance of fathers to their daughters*. Focus on the Family. https://www.focusonthefamily.com/parenting/importance-of-fathers-to-their-daughters/

Sciequan, D. C. (2023). *The role of father involvement in the perceived psychological well-being of daughters with a focus on women of color* [Doctoral dissertation, Liberty University]. ScholarsCrossing. https://digitalcommons.liberty.edu/cgi/viewcontent.cgi?article=5789&context=doctoral

Secunda, V. (n.d.). In Lemire, S. (2024, June 12), *78 father-daughter quotes that speak to their unbreakable bond.* Today. https://www.today.com/life/holidays/father-daughter-quotes-rcna27545

Sexton, A. (n.d.). In Lemire, S. (2024, June 12), *78 father-daughter quotes that speak to their unbreakable bond.* Today. https://www.today.com/life/holidays/father-daughter-quotes-rcna27545

Shafer, K. (2021, June 20). Nurturing dads raise emotionally intelligent kids - helping make society more respectful and equitable. *Iowa Capital Dispatch.* https://iowacapitaldispatch.com/2021/06/20/nurturing-dads-raise-emotionally-intelligent-kids-helping-make-society-more-respectful-and-equitable/

Shalders, S. (2020, May 28). *5 things dads can do to raise emotionally healthy children.* The Centre for Perinatal Health and Parenting. https://www.perinatalhealth.com.au/blog/5-things-dads-can-do-to-raise-emotionally-healthy-children-1

Sibley, D. S., & Granger, K. (2019, July 15). *How fathers influence their daughters' romantic relationships.* https://ifstudies.org/blog/how-fathers-influence-their-daughters-romantic-relationships

The significance of a father's influence. (n.d.). Focus on the Family. https://www.focusonthefamily.com/family-qa/the-significance-of-a-fathers-influence/

Sindall, O. (2021, September 11). *The dad effect: Staying connected to teen and tween daughters.* Twixt. https://www.wearetwixt.com/post/the-dad-effect-staying-connected-to-tween-and-teen-daughters

Soutter, F. (2024, July 16). *8 ways fathers can empower their daughters.* Amitie Lane. https://amitielane.com/blogs/raising-empowered-girls/8-ways-fathers-can-empower-their-daughters?_pos=1&_sid=0d1907a09&_ss=r

Stade, L. (2022, August 27). *10 tips for building better father-daughter relationships.* Linda Stade Education. https://lindastade.com/building-father-daughter-relationships/

Starrick, S. (2023, June 16). *A father's vital role in teaching children empathy and emotional intelligence.* Jai Institute for Parenting. https://www.jaiinstituteforparenting.com/a-fathers-vital-role-in-teaching-children-empathy-and-emotional-intelligence

Statistics tell the story: Fathers matter. (n.d.) National Fatherhood Initiative. https://www.fatherhood.org/father-absence-statistic

Strait, G. (n.d.). In Lemire, S. (2024, June 12), *78 father-daughter quotes that speak to their unbreakable bond.* Today. https://www.today.com/life/holidays/father-daughter-quotes-rcna27545

Strauss Cohen, I. (2017, July 23). *How to achieve emotional success.* Psychology Today. https://www.psychologytoday.com/us/blog/your-emotional-meter/201707/how-to-achieve-emotional-success

Suizzo, M., Rackley, K. R., Robbins, P. A., Jackson, K. M., Rarick, J. R. D., & McClain, S. (2016, November 16). The unique effects of fathers' warmth on adolescents' positive beliefs and behaviors: Pathways to resilience in low-income families. *Sex Roles, 77*, 46-58. https://doi.org/10.1007/s11199-016-0696-9

Suzy. (2022, September 28). How to have meaningful conversations with your adult kids. *Empty Nest Blessed.* https://emptynestblessed.com/2022/09/28/meaningful-conversations-adult-kids/

Swindoll, C. R. (n.d.). In Lemire, S. (2024, June 12), *78 father-daughter quotes that speak to their unbreakable bond.* Today. https://www.today.com/life/holidays/father-daughter-quotes-rcna27545

Tabrez, H. (2023, March 30). Family man: A father's guide to raising emotionally stable children. *Gulf News.* https://gulfnews.com/parenting/mums-dads/family-man-a-fathers-guide-to-raising-emotionally-stable-children-1.1680096828414

Ten tasks of adolescent development. (n.d.). Raising Teens. https://hr.mit.edu/static/worklife/raising-teens/ten-tasks.html

Tift, J. N. (2019, December 20). *A father's place: the importance of male involvement in early childhood development, in partnership with Region 9 Head Start Association.* Continued. https://www.continued.com/early-childhood-education/articles/father-s-place-importance-male-23357

25 dad and daughter activities to try this year. (n.d.). Daily Mom. https://dailymom.com/nurture/25-dad-daughter-activities-to-try/

Vanchugova, D., Norman, H., & Elliot, M. J. (2022, November). Measuring the association between fathers' involvement and risky behaviours in adolescence. *Social Science Research, 108,* 102749. https://doi.org/10.1016/j.ssresearch.2022.102749

Vinopal, L. (2019, July 22). *How fathers of daughters can help women make more money.* Ladders. https://www.theladders.com/career-advice/how-fathers-of-daughters-can-help-women-make-more-money

Watson, M. (n.d.). *Just speak to your daughter's heart.* Fathers.com. https://fathers.com/blog/your-kids/daughters/just-speak-to-your-daughters-heart-just-be-dad/

Watson Canfield, M. (2016, January 22). The dialed-in dad checklist: Your fathering self-assessment. *Dr. Michelle Watson Canfield.* https://www.drmichellewatson.com/blog/2016/1/21/the-dialed-in-dad-checklist-your-fathering-self-assessment

What are the 5 love languages? (n.d.). Love Languages. https://5lovelanguages.com/learn

What is active listening? (2024, September 1). Center for Creative Leadership. https://www.ccl.org/articles/leading-effectively-articles/coaching-others-use-active-listening-skills/

Why routines are good for your health. (n.d.). Piedmont. https://www.piedmont.org/living-real-change/why-routines-are-good-for-your-health

Williams, A. (2021, February 7). *How I overcame emotional neglect.* The Fatherless Daughters. https://thefatherlessdaughters.com/2021/02/07/how-i-overcame-emotional-neglect/

Wilson, D., & Wilson, A. (Hosts). (2021, April 20). Communication tips for dads with their daughters [Audio podcast episode]. In *FamilyLife Today*. FamilyLife Today. https://www.familylife.com/podcast/familylife-today/communication-tips-for-dads-with-their-daughters/

Winston, R., & Chicot, R. (2016). The importance of early bonding on the long-term mental health and resilience of children. *London Journal of Primary Care, 8*(1), 12–14. https://doi.org/10.1080/17571472.2015.1133012

Witmer Jr., K. D. (2021, April 1). Fatherhood: Set age-appropriate boundaries and maintain them. *Coastal Point.* https://www.coastalpoint.com/opinion/experts_corner/fatherhood-set-age-appropriate-boundaries-and-maintain-them/article_a01b2e50-90cf-11eb-9cf1-83291a37d4e4.html

Wolf, K. (2022, June 18). *Harvard-trained parenting expert: Fathers who do these 8 things are more likely to raise confident, strong-minded daughters.* CNBC Make It. https://www.cnbc.com/2022/06/18/harvard-trained-parenting-expert-shares-signs-of-a-healthy-father-daughter-relationship.html

Work-life balance: Tips for you and your family. (n.d.). Raisingchildren.net.au. https://raisingchildren.net.au/grown-ups/work-child-care/worklife-balance/work-life-balance

Wright, J. S. (2017, March 10). *Out of the fog: A personal story of verbal abuse.* Medium. https://medium.com/@jswright/out-of-the-fog-a-personal-story-of-verbal-abuse-cf570530305d

Yassin, F. (2023, September 6). *Attachment theory: How the father-child relationship shapes a young person's life.* The Wave Clinic. https://thewaveclinic.com/blog/attachment-theory-how-father-child-relationship-shapes-life/

Zalis, S. (2019, June 16). *Female leaders on lessons learned from their fathers.* Forbes. https://www.forbes.com/sites/shelleyzalis/2019/06/15/female-leaders-on-lessons-learned-from-their-fathers/

www.ingramcontent.com/pod-product-compliance
Lightning Source LLC
Chambersburg PA
CBHW061604110426
42742CB00039B/2820